"Suzanne Crocker has served as a missionary in West Africa for ten years. Along with her husband, John, she has shared the gospel and planted churches while effectively ministering to suffering and human need through her personal medical ministry. However, there is another side to missionary life. The challenge of cross-cultural adjustments and demands of an austere lifestyle create situations that are embarrassing, humorous, and opportunities for growth. *Pig in a Taxi and Other African Adventures* will be amusing and enjoyable reading for anyone interested in missionary life. But Crocker's writing is more than entertaining. Out of each anecdote is a spiritual lesson to be learned and insight into how to pray for missionaries in a more practical and relevant way."

Jerry Rankin, president, International Mission Board

"*Pig in a Taxi and Other African Adventures* captured my heart. I was like a sponge, taking it in from cover to cover. I couldn't put it down. It reflects a marvelous insight into mission life. I laughed, I cried, I rejoiced, and I praised the Lord. Having enjoyed the privilege of participating in four short-term mission encounters with the Crockers in Togo and Benin, West Africa, I found that reading of their adventures added to my awareness of what it must be like to walk in missionary shoes. It enhanced my appreciation and love for all Great Commission champions. I would encourage everyone to secure a copy of Suzanne's refreshing book. Reading it will 'step up' your intercessory prayer for missionaries. It will encourage increased involvement and investment in global missions. And you'll be glad!"

Dick Thomassian, president, Training in Mission Evangelism (TIME)

"The book *Pig in a Taxi and Other African Adventures* by Suzanne Crocker is a wonderful read. I have been reading books for seventy-five plus years, and this is one of my favorites. It will appeal to all ages. It is a must-read for all who are considering missionary service, either short-term or career. They will definitely profit by reading the book."

B. Gray Allison, president emeritus,
Mid-America Baptist Theological Seminary

"Suzanne is a wonderful person. She is as transparent in real life as anyone with whom I am acquainted. Her serious and yet lighthearted way of telling a story makes for easy reading. As a devotional-type book, *Pig in a Taxi and Other African Adventures* has a novel emphasis on practical application that is refreshing. However, I think Suzanne's greatest strength is the unique way in which she appeals to the reader to think about missionaries as real people with real needs."

Dr. Jimmy E. Jackson, senior pastor, Whitesburg Baptist Church

PIG in a TAXI

and Other African Adventures

Suzanne Crocker

Grand Rapids, Michigan

Published by Baker Books
a division of Baker Publishing Group
P.O. Box 6287, Grand Rapids, MI 49516-6287

Printed in the United States of America

Library of Congress Cataloging-in-Publication Data
Crocker, Suzanne.
Pig in a taxi and other African adventures / Suzanne Crocker.
p. cm.
Includes bibliographical references.
ISBN 10: 0-8010-6632-8 (pbk.)
ISBN 978-0-8010-6632-0 (pbk).
1. Crocker, Suzanne. 2. Missionaries—Africa—Biography. 3. Missionaries—United States—Biography. 4. Missionaries—Religious life. I. Title.
BV3705.C76A3 2006
266′.02373066—dc22 2006003330

I lovingly dedicate this book to my family. John, you have been a faithful husband to me for seventeen years. Thank you for encouraging me to pursue this dream of writing a book. Sarah Joy, Rebekah, Christopher, and Benjamin, being your mom is a dream come true. I love you very much.

Contents

Acknowledgments

This series of stories is a sampling of fifteen years of adventure for our family. There are many people through those years who have encouraged us, taught us, and lived these stories with us.

First of all, I would like to thank my husband and children for their willingness to allow me to put them in the spotlight and share an inside view of our family. You are all a source of much joy and laughter in my days.

I would like to thank my mother-in-law for encouraging me to write these stories and giving me deadlines. If not for her gentle push, this book would still be just an idea that I would have liked to do someday when the kids are grown. You have prodded and encouraged me every step of the way, and I am grateful.

My parents, John and Nancy Laramore, encouraged me and believed in me. Thank you for telling me that I could write and for believing in me for all these years. My brother, Phil Laramore, encouraged me simply by surviving terrible tragedy and turning it into victory. You taught me to persevere through your example.

Judy Miller and Kathy Daniels played a very real part in this book since they have been the ones responsible for safely evacuating us during our medical and civil war crises.

LaVerne Brown has been willing to give four years of her life here in Togo teaching my children and enabling us to remain here longer than we first thought we would.

Edith Friesen, you have been a dear friend, encourager, nurse, and helper throughout the last few years. Truly "better a neighbor nearby than a brother far away" (Prov. 27:10). There have been many times in the last few years when I might not have made it without your listening ear and kind words.

Our many friends and colleagues with the International Mission Board and other missions have lived these stories with us. I hope you see yourselves in these pages and laugh as you remember those times.

Introduction

I watched the movie with tears streaming down my cheeks. The closing line was, "She never came back to Africa." My friends kept trying to console me, but I just cried on and on. What if I never came back to Africa? It was the end of summer. I was in Sanyati, Zimbabwe, where I had served as a summer missionary. I was nineteen years old. The next day I would start the journey that would carry me back to the United States and my sophomore year of college.

It had been one of the best summers of my life. Most of my life I had felt that God wanted me to be a missionary nurse in Africa. I had made all my major decisions in light of that fact, but there was always a question below the surface: what if I get there and hate it? I had seen a volunteer position available to be a summer missionary in Sanyati and jumped at the chance. Not only was it an opportunity to test my call to Africa and see if the continent really did fit me well, but it was also where my best friend lived. Her mother would be my supervisor, and I would eat all my meals with her family. It seemed too good to be true. What better way to find out if this was really for me?

When I arrived Mrs. Randall told me that the government had turned down the Bible project I was supposed to work on, but she was sure she and the other missionaries on the mission station could find something for me to do. I was initially disappointed, but as soon as I went to the mission hospital I knew that it had worked out for the best. I had completed my first year of nursing school, which meant I had some head knowledge but no actual experience in nursing. I had never even given an injection before. When I showed up at the hospital the staff took me under their collective wings and put me to work. Their first job was to teach me to drink hot tea, because you can't work at the hospital without tea time! By the end of the summer I was hooked on both hot tea and missionary medical work.

The hospital staff taught me how to do many things. That summer I not only gave thousands of shots at well baby clinics (a place set up in the bush where mothers can bring their babies on a monthly basis for vaccinations, weight checks, and advice on caring for children; it is designed to lower the infant mortality rate), but I also learned how to do minor surgery, to deliver babies, and to do many other important jobs at the perpetually understaffed hospital. It was a wonderful summer when I learned that I really could do all things through Christ who gives me strength (see Phil. 4:13). Not only was missionary nursing in Africa a perfect fit jobwise for me, but I also loved it and I loved Africa. This was where I wanted to spend the rest of my life.

Now my summer was coming to an end, and the movie had hit on my biggest fear: what if I never got to come back? As you can tell from this book, though, I did come back to Africa many times. It has become my home and the place where my family has grown up.

During my summer in Zimbabwe I corresponded with a friend from college who was a summer missionary in Israel. I knew he also felt called to Africa as a missionary, and I wanted to share my experiences with him. Little did I know that less than two years later we would be married and preparing to go to Africa together.

John and I married December 17, 1988. We began seminary just a few weeks later in Columbia, South Carolina. We were young and impatient, and we did not understand why mission boards required so much education. About three months into our seminary experience we were accepted by a small, independent mission board. We began raising support and left for the mission field in October 1989. We were all of twenty-three and twenty-one years old, idealistic, energetic, and ready to take on the world. The first dozen stories in this book are about that time period. At that point we lived in a village without electricity and part of the time without water. We stayed for only eight months, as we realized there was a reason most of the larger mission boards had their educational requirements. We then returned to the United States.

We immediately went to seminary. This time John attended Mid-America Baptist Theological Seminary and earned his Master of Divinity degree. We spent several very productive years there, and during that time God blessed us with both Sarah Joy and Rebekah, our first two adopted children. Then we were accepted by the International Mission Board of the SBC (Southern Baptist Convention) as International Service Corps missionaries. This was a two-year program where we gained experience before becoming career missionaries. After our ISC term we returned as career missionaries and have continued through the present time.

In this book I've tried to share with you some of what I have learned along the way and how it applies to life in America as well as in Africa. I hope to be an encouragement and to bring some laughter into your life. So please read on and be encouraged.

Part 1

Life in Lassa Bas

(1989–1990)

Thanksgiving Fiasco

> Man looks at the outward appearance, but the Lord looks at the heart.
>
> 1 Samuel 16:7

It was both my first Thanksgiving in Africa and my first Thanksgiving as a married woman. I wanted everything to be absolutely perfect. Our mission director and his wife were coming for lunch, and I was determined to replicate the American Thanksgiving meal as closely as possible. However, it was hot and dusty and didn't seem like Thanksgiving. There were no fall leaves, pilgrim hats, colorful decorations, or even frozen turkeys. Yet I was determined to find substitutes for everything.

While shopping in the market I had found a pumpkin-like gourd that I was sure would do for pumpkin pie. Our house help kept insisting that it was a fruit and couldn't be made into pie, but I would not be deterred. It was orange, shaped like a long, thin pumpkin, and smelled somewhat like a pumpkin, so I was sure it would work. Later I saw a lady going down the road carrying a basin full of field corn on her head. It had not been dried yet, so I knew I could convert it into creamed corn. The pièce de résistance was two fat roosters purchased from the widows who lived on our premises. I asked our helper, Cockoo, to kill and clean the roosters while I worked on the rest of the meal. He set to work and in a short period of time brought me two plucked and lovely roosters. He assured me they were completely clean and ready to roast. I didn't want to hurt his feelings by inspecting his work too closely, so I sprinkled some herbs on the birds and popped them into the oven.

Our director and his wife had never celebrated Thanksgiving in Togo since they didn't think it was worth the fuss. Yet they were delighted with our invitation and came to share this special occasion with us. The table setting was beautiful with sparkling china and a lacy tablecloth. The food looked delicious: creamed corn, crisp green beans, savory dressing, pumpkin pie, and two lovely, lightly browned roosters. We thanked the Lord for our blessings and asked our director to carve the rooster. As he cut into the first bird his facial expression turned into one of puzzlement and then disgust. Our lovely birds still had all their intestines and "stuff" inside and were only partially cooked.

We had a delightful vegetarian Thanksgiving that year.

What about you? How many of us are like those roosters—lovely on the outside but filled with bad stuff on the inside? Ask God to transform your heart and cleanse you of any internal sins such as pride, mean-spiritedness, callousness toward others, and so forth.

Missionary Prayer Point: Pray that missionaries would truly seek after God and let him clean up their hearts. Pray that they would be aware of any internal sins and be open to the leading of the Holy Spirit as he cleans them from the inside out.

Things That Go Bump in the Night

> Even the darkness will not be dark to you; the night will shine like the day, for darkness is as light to you.
>
> Psalm 139:12

We definitely weren't in Kansas anymore. As zealous and eager as we were to come to Africa, we were ill equipped to deal with the realities of life without running water and electricity. Simple things we had taken for granted, like bathing, became hardships. I was tired of standing in the shower and scooping water one meager cupful at a time to pour over myself and scrub. I wanted to submerge at least part of my hot, tired, and dirty body into some water and soak. It didn't seem like much to wish for. My sweet husband went to the market and bought a large basin that women use for hauling water, and then he filled it with cool water. I was ecstatic. I submerged as much of myself as I possibly could and settled in for a nice long soak. It was simply delightful—until I tried to get out.

That was when my problem began. I had not considered the force of suction. I was completely stuck to the bottom of the basin, and no amount of pulling and prying would get me out. I finally had to stand up with the basin still stuck to me and water running all over the floor before John could pry it loose. Needless to say, after cleaning up all that mess my bucket shower looked a little more inviting.

And I never did get accustomed to the total darkness of a night in a village without electricity. It seemed like our flashlights always had dead batteries, and many creatures loved the darkness. Several times I was in bed trying to read by candlelight and John would say, "Stay still—don't turn around!" Then he would kill a scorpion that was crawling up the wall by my head.

One night I got up to go to the bathroom. I lit the only candle in our room and carried it with me. When I pushed the bathroom door open a mouse jumped on me. I did what any red-blooded American female would have done: I dropped my candle and screamed at the top of my lungs. My candle went out and my scream woke up John. The only thing he knew was that his wife was somewhere in the dark screaming and he had no light. I cautiously navigated my way back to the bedroom, knowing that the mouse was out in the darkness somewhere. Once I reassured John that there wasn't a burglar in the house and told him my mouse tale, we had a good laugh. Then I asked him to come with me in case the mouse was still lurking in the dark waiting to attack.

In spite of all the inconveniences and minor disasters, God was teaching us to wait on him. His angels were around us and were protecting us even in the darkness. The darkness that frightened me was as light as day to my Savior who was watching over me.

What about you? Does your life seem dark, and do you wonder if God still sees you? Trust in him. He is watching over you and protecting you, whatever your circumstances may be.

Missionary Prayer Point: Pray that missionaries would really sense God's watchful presence in their lives. Pray that God would keep them safe and light their way.

Me, Drive a Stick Shift?

I can do everything through him who gives me strength.

Philippians 4:13

It wasn't that John hadn't tried. He really had made a valiant effort. Before we came to the mission field, we knew that our vehicle would be a stick shift, so he tried to teach me how to drive it. We borrowed a friend's vehicle and hopped all around the campus at our seminary. Our lessons always ended with John frustrated and me in tears. I could not seem to get the hang of three pedals instead of two. We decided that the simplest thing would be to let John drive while we were on the mission field. After all, where would I be going without him? We were newlyweds with no children and couldn't imagine not doing everything together on this big adventure.

Let me give a little background on my driving history. I had renewed my learner's permit four times since I didn't see the point of getting my driver's license. My little brother drove, and between him, my parents, and my friends there was always someone going wherever I needed to go. Why should I drive if someone could drive me around? Finally as a sophomore in college I was confronted with the need to get to the hospital before 6:30 a.m. for nursing class. No one was eager to drive me anywhere at that hour, so I took a driver's education class and got my license. I was a licensed driver but definitely not a driving fiend.

When John and I arrived in Togo, a new, beautiful silver Daihatsu Rocky was waiting for us. It was a stick shift, and the four-wheel drive helped us get through many tough village roads. Initially, our plan worked beautifully. John drove us to all the clinics. He enjoyed driving, and the challenging terrain made getting to work more of an adventure than a chore.

I never counted on the fact that one day John might be sick and need something. But one fateful day that very thing happened. He was hot and tired and feeling miserable. He looked up at me and said, "I would give anything for something cold to drink." Without electricity there was certainly nothing cold to drink at our house, but I knew there was a town seven kilometers away with restaurants and refrigeration. I decided that with God's help, I could do anything, even drive our SUV. I called our cook to come get in the car, and off we went.

I won't say that it was a smooth ride. In fact, Cockoo's eyes became as big as saucers and he fearfully told me, "Mama, the car doesn't do this when Mr. Missionary drives!" Nevertheless, we hopped into town, obtained some cold drinks, and made our way back home. By the time we got back I had the hang of it, and I've been driving all over West Africa ever since.

What about you? Are there any skills that you have been afraid to develop or new things you have been afraid to try? As Christians, we truly can do all things through Christ who gives us strength. Take your strength from him and try something new. You'll be amazed at what you can do through him.

Missionary Prayer Point: Pray for missionaries to be willing to develop new skills that will help them both in their job and in their personal day-to-day life. Pray that they would not grow stagnant but would be constantly learning and growing through Christ's strength.

The Language-Learning Blues

> Utterly amazed, they asked: "Are not all these men who are speaking Galileans? Then how is it that each of us hears them in his own native language?"
>
> Acts 2:7–8

One of the most daunting tasks that every missionary faces is learning to communicate with the people they have come to serve. Often there are no language schools or trained teachers. You have to find someone willing to teach you and then train them how to teach you—without speaking a word of their language. It definitely seems overwhelming at times. We often prayed that God would miraculously allow us to speak to the people of Togo clearly and in their own language as the apostles did at Pentecost, but God had many lessons to teach us through the process of learning the language. So no miracle occurred; we simply studied, worked, and stumbled our way into learning how to communicate with the people of Togo and Benin. Years later my daughter Sarah Joy would walk down the road with her mouth open. I fussed at her for not politely greeting people as we met them on the road. She simply pointed to her open mouth and said, "See, no French will come out." Oh, how I wished that French would simply come out freely and understandably just because our mouths were open.

John and I have learned (or at least attempted to learn) three languages since being on the mission field: French, Kabiye, and Ditamari. Initially we made a perfect team. I could fairly quickly comprehend a language but not really speak it, and John could speak it but not understand a word that is being said to him. Of course, we could eventually both speak and understand, but there were some interesting moments in those initial months. Once during that time, we left our clinic to find an attractive woman standing by our car with her bags packed and holding a toddler. She proceeded to tell John, "I don't think it is right that a great man like you should have only one wife. I've packed up my bags and my son and am ready to come with you and be your second wife."

John, believing that she had just asked for a ride, invited her to hop in the car. I promptly interpreted what she had actually said, and we went home without a passenger.

What about you? Do you struggle with communicating with those around you? Maybe you feel disconnected from teenagers or don't know quite how to relate to an older generation. Our God can transcend all language, generational, and cultural barriers. Seek to develop relationships with others who are different from you. Pray that God would help you find points of common interest as your life is enriched by others who may speak a different "language" than you do.

Missionary Prayer Point: Pray for missionaries to maintain their perspective and the ability to laugh at themselves as they learn new cultures and languages. Pray that they would become fluent in the languages they work in and be able to clearly share the love of Christ with those around them.

Eating My Way to Peace and Quiet

> When Jesus heard what had happened, he withdrew by boat privately to a solitary place.
>
> Matthew 14:13

Pintards, otherwise known as West African guinea fowl, are some of the noisiest creatures that God ever created. They are beautiful, colorful birds, but they are so nervous. They are constantly squawking and worrying about something. They seem perpetually anxious and make so much more noise than a plain old-fashioned chicken. In fact, they are such nervous, distractible birds that they make terrible mothers. Such a large number of their offspring die that it is unprofitable to raise them. Farmers in Togo have learned to give the guinea fowl eggs to a hen to sit on. When the eggs hatch, the hen makes an excellent mother, teaching her chicks how to scratch for food and protecting them. It is funny to see a mama hen with a brood of nervous guinea chicks almost as big as she is. She often looks as if she is thinking, "How in the world did I make such funny-looking children?"

At our house in Lassa Bas we struggled with a lack of privacy and the constant noise level. When we arranged to rent that house, there were three widows who lived on the premises. Since they lived in outside buildings and not in the portion of the house we were going to inhabit, we felt that it would be fine for them to continue living there. I mean, what new missionary is going to evict three widows from her property? Unfortunately, we didn't consider all that was entailed in that decision. Those three older ladies came with grown children, goats, chickens, and a whole flock of very nervous guinea fowl. We could never lock our gate because we had people living in the courtyard. Thus we had a constant stream of visitors coming to gawk at us.

We had been married less than a year, and the constant lack of privacy was really frustrating. One Saturday morning we decided that we had worked hard all week and were going to sleep late regardless of what the village thought. About six a.m. there was a loud knock on the door. I whispered to John, "Ignore it. They'll eventually go away." The knocking got louder and louder, but we were determined to ignore it. Finally it stopped, and we settled down to have a good sleep. Just then we jumped as a loud voice came from the open window: "Are you okay in there? You're not answering your door!" The jig was up. There was nothing left to do but open the door and deal with our visitor.

I couldn't do anything about the early-morning visitors, but I decided that I would be a more pleasant, rested, and energetic missionary if those silly guinea fowl would be quiet. They roosted on a branch right outside our bedroom window. All night long they would clatter and chatter at intervals. At four a.m. they were up for the day and felt that the rest of the world should be too. They would squawk and make such a racket that no one could sleep. The more I was awakened, the more I fumed about those birds. Then I had a brilliant idea—I would eat my way to peace and quiet. Every week I would buy one of those guineas from the old ladies and eat it for supper. Within a few months there would be peace and quiet in the Crocker yard.

The ladies were delighted to sell one of their birds. I gleefully watched Cockoo kill and clean it. One less pintard was in the yard. A few days later it seemed like there were just as many guineas as before. Surely I had simply miscounted. I bought another bird and another and another. Instead of getting quieter, the yard seemed to be getting noisier. I just didn't understand.

After a few weeks it dawned on me what was happening: selling guineas to me was so profitable that every time I bought one bird, the older ladies would replace it with two. I finally realized that I would never be able to eat my way to peace and quiet.

I never did completely adjust to the lack of privacy or the noise level, but I learned to treasure moments of quietness and peace. Sometimes at night the animals would be asleep, the candles would be lit, and a cool, gentle breeze would blow through the mosquito net. We learned how to hold on to those precious moments of silence and let them renew and restore us for the bustle of the coming day.

What about you? You probably aren't dealing with guinea fowl in your yard, but you may be caught up in the noise and bustle of daily life. Seek out times of quietness and allow God to renew your spirit so you can face the coming day.

Missionary Prayer Point: Pray for missionaries to find a quiet place where they can be alone with God. Pray that they would make this quietness foundational in their busy and noisy lives.

Missionary Meals

> Then a voice told him, "Get up, Peter. Kill and eat."
> "Surely not, Lord!" Peter replied. "I have never eaten anything impure or unclean."
>
> Acts 10:13–14

"Where he leads me, I will follow. What he feeds me, I will swallow." This was our tongue-in-cheek approach to some of the foods we would eat on the mission field. When I initially began clinics in Togo, the villagers wanted to give us something in return for the medicine, so they would prepare a meal for us in the middle of the clinic day. There was no way to politely refuse the meal, no matter how unappealing it might be. We were very rarely left to eat our meal in peace. Everyone wanted to watch us and be sure we were enjoying their food. Sometimes the food was very good. Our favorite meal was a rice-and-red-sauce dish. It was spicy enough to cause you to break into a sweat but palatable nonetheless. We appreciated the sacrifice people made to feed us when we went to the village, and we understood that they didn't want to just receive from us, they wanted to give us what they could. However, it was easier to receive those gifts of food on some days than others.

One day we sat down to eat the meal prepared for us only to find it was cold, leftover foufou with a sauce made of boiled okra and fish. It was extremely slimy. For the uninitiated, let me describe foufou. It is a tasteless mound of starch made from pounded yams that has the texture of mashed potatoes mixed with glue. Now, many years and many pots later, I genuinely enjoy foufou with a good sauce, but initially it was difficult to consume. As I have heard many missionaries say, "It is a texture thing." We just don't have any foods that have exactly the same texture.

We took our place at the communal dish and began to eat our foufou. I was very nonchalantly avoiding the fish and simply dipping my foufou into the sauce and eating it. I'm not a fish fan to begin with, and cold fish that had been boiled with okra was too much for me.

About halfway through the meal the chief's son looked at me and in an accusatory manner said, "You don't like our food!"

"Of course I do. Don't you see me eating?"

"You haven't eaten any fish this whole meal," he insisted. With every eye fixed on me, I blindly reached into the pot and pulled out the prized delicacy—the fish head with eyeballs and all looking back at me. There was no graceful way out, so I ate my fish head while making appreciative sounds. Sometimes it is very difficult to be grateful for the food we are given!

What about you? Do you live a life of conscious gratitude to our Creator for the daily blessings of food that he gives us? Make an effort today to be genuinely thankful for what we have to eat, from broccoli to chocolate. It is all a gift of his abundant goodness toward us.

Missionary Prayer Point: Pray for missionaries to have a grateful heart for the provision God has given them. Pray also for protection from amoebas and other parasites that may be lurking in their food. Pray that missionaries would be creative and able to cook appetizing meals for their families from locally available ingredients.

Abide

> And who knows but that you have come to royal position for such a time as this?
>
> Esther 4:14

Typically we would have a village clinic one day and then return to the same place to hold a Bible study on the following day. We usually had about three clinics in a week. I had five villages that I circulated among in a regular fashion. Usually the clinic was extremely crowded on clinic days, and then on the Bible study days a fair number of people would come to see what we were all about. One day we had driven about an hour to Koudjoukadaa to hold the Bible study, and no one had shown up. Not only had no one shown up for the Bible study, but even the streets were empty.

Finally someone came and told us that one of the wives of the chief had died, and everyone was at the funeral. I immediately knew who the person was. One of my regular patients was a forty-six-year-old woman who had recently given birth to her tenth child. In a country where the average life span is only fifty-two years, being forty-six is old, far too old to be giving birth. Over the last month we had watched both mother and baby grow weaker in spite of our best efforts. We had done everything we possibly could, but it wasn't enough.

We went to the chief's home to offer our condolences. While we were talking I asked, "What about the baby?" You see, in the village there was no milk or formula available, and baby Abide's mother had been carrying her from woman to woman to beg them to nurse her a little. Now there was no one to care for Abide. (Ironically, her name meant "queen" or "rich woman.") Abide had been placed alone in a room during the funeral because no one wanted to hear her cry. Typically a funeral lasts about three days, and there was no way she could survive that long.

With the chief's blessing we brought Abide home with us to Kara. I had my doubts that she would even survive the two-hour drive because she was so weak and dehydrated. She was a month old and weighed less than five pounds. In spite of everything, God had saved her life for a very special purpose. Just as he had placed a young Jewish girl, Esther, in a royal palace in Susa to save her people from the butchery of Haman, so God had a very special plan for baby Abide's life.

What about you? One person can't save the whole world, and it is easy to become overwhelmed by all the needs you encounter. However, you can make an impact on the world one life at a time. Open your eyes to the needs of others around you and be open to God's leading. You never know how you may be able to impact another person simply by being available.

Missionary Prayer Point: Pray for missionaries who experience heart-wrenching situations on a daily basis. Pray for them to be courageous and not to grow callous to the pain around them.

God's Provision for Abide

> And my God will meet all your needs according to his glorious riches in Christ Jesus.
>
> Philippians 4:19

We made it back into town with Abide and now faced the challenge of what and how we were going to feed this baby. We stopped at the store and found one bottle in stock. We promptly bought it. Of course there was no formula available to buy, but I had a village health-care book that had a recipe for baby formula. We bought the ingredients for the formula as well. Then we hunted all over the market for diapers and diaper pins. We thought different ladies at the market might have one or two Chinese diapers for sale. They looked like little terry-cloth towels, but you didn't use diaper pins; you tied a plastic cover over each one to keep it on the baby. We finally managed to accumulate about a dozen diapers.

We carried Abide home and began to feed her. Initially she was too weak to suck on a bottle, so we fed her with a medicine dropper. By the second or third feeding she was ready to latch on to that bottle. She really began to thrive. It seemed as if overnight she grew from a sickly, four-and-a-half-pound baby to a healthy, giggly, thirteen-pound baby. Amazingly, she did not seem to suffer from any significant developmental delays. She quickly became the light of our lives. She was so precious and such an integral part of our little family.

When Abide was about four months old we were nearing the time for our return to the United States, so we went with Abide to visit her family and discuss her future. The family was very supportive of the idea of us adopting her. However, when we contacted the American Embassy, we found out that we did not have enough time left in the country to legally adopt her. We knew a Togolese co-worker, a national pastor, who was childless. He and his wife had been praying for a child for over ten years and had fallen in love with Abide. So with the permission of the chief and his family, Abide moved in with Pastor Issifou and his wife when we left the country.

I thought my heart would break when we said good-bye, but many years later I met Abide again with her family. She was a plump, healthy, and polite young woman. She was an excellent student and loved God wholeheartedly. The chief had agreed that Issifou could raise Abide until she was a teenager. Then she had to return to her village to marry there. When Pastor and Mrs. Issifou brought her back so we could return to the village, everything within me cried out, "This is wrong!" Abide loved her family. She was accustomed to living in town with a Christian family. How would she ever adapt to life in a pagan village living with people who were strangers to her and be expected to marry as a young teenager?

I shouldn't have worried. Issifou showed the wisdom of Solomon in dealing with the chief. He presented his daughter and showed how well cared for she had been. Then he gave the chief a list of all the expenses related to twelve years of care and said he would be glad for the chief to reimburse him since the chief now wanted the girl back. The chief quickly changed his mind about taking back Abide and said he could see she was loved and well cared for. He decreed that she could be Issifou's daughter permanently. We all rejoiced, knowing Abide was safe and would never be separated from her parents now.

Seeing Abide again secure and happy with her family caused me to realize that God's plan and provision for her had been the best. She had grown into a confident and godly young woman. Guess what name her adoptive parents had given her? Esther!

What about you? Do you have needs that seem insurmountable? We serve a great God who has resources we can't even imagine. Trust God to meet your needs. His plan is always best.

Missionary Prayer Point: Pray for missionaries to clearly sense God's direction in every situation that they face. Pray that they would see God's abundant provision for their every need.

Doctor Wannabe

> It is not the healthy who need a doctor, but the sick. I have not come to call the righteous, but sinners to repentance.
>
> Luke 5:31–32

I had been a registered nurse for a grand total of about a year. I was twenty-one years old and ready to take on the world. My job in Togo was to provide health care for five villages that had no access to health care while John planted churches and trained leaders. I had a book titled *Where There Is No Doctor*, a good supply of medicine, and a willing heart.

First we made the rounds of the five villages that had been assigned to us. My initial thought was, *How will we ever find these places again?* The villages were well off the main road. In fact, most of them were down small trails that crossed fields and bore no resemblance to any road I had ever seen. There certainly weren't any street signs to give us directions. After we had been introduced to the chiefs and learned our route, we set up a village visitation schedule and went to work.

Our clinics were held in all sorts of structures, from a thatch gazebo to a nice cinder block building with a tin roof. Each village provided a place for us to have the clinic. Typically we would arrive at a village by eight a.m. and treat people all day long. We could usually treat one hundred to two hundred people in a day's time. As word spread, more and more people would come. At the end of the day there were usually more people in line than there had been at the beginning of the day. It was a never-ending task.

It was definitely a time of culture shock and of learning a lot about different tribes and their perceptions of various illnesses. One day I had a mother who kept insisting that her daughter was allergic to the moon. This challenged my diagnostic skills because none of my books had a listing under the topic of "moon allergy." After asking a myriad of questions, a pattern became clear. The child had high fevers every night, and since the fevers came just after nightfall, the family assumed that they were caused by the moon. We treated the child for malaria, and before long she was well.

Another time a parent told me she didn't know what kind of a demon was coming out of her child's tooth. It seemed to be developing a big black crater to let the evil spirit out. The crater was simply a cavity.

We tried helping people who were suffering with everything from malaria and parasites to wounds and burns. We provided prenatal care to many women and did health teaching to help them prevent many of the common illnesses that plagued them. It was never enough, but we genuinely tried to help as many as we could, and God blessed our efforts.

What about you? Do you put off certain jobs because you feel inadequate or incapable of doing them well? Trust God to equip you for any job he asks you to do. As inadequate as I often felt, I was serving the Master Healer, and he equipped me day by day for what I needed to do. He'll do the same for you as you depend on him.

Missionary Prayer Point: Pray for missionaries to be willing to take risks and to try serving in new ways. Pray that God would strengthen and equip them to do the task he has called them to do.

Part 2

Life as an International Service Corps Volunteer

(1995–1996)

Bunnies

> The earth is the LORD's, and everything in it, the world, and all who live in it.
>
> Psalm 24:1

We had returned to the mission field and were living in town with running water and electricity. We could not believe the difference it made in both our comfort level and our productivity. We loved our clean, new duplex, but it did have some peculiarities. One of our favorites was the fact that the living room/dining room was separated from the kitchen and bedrooms by a small breezeway. To carry dinner to the table you actually walked outside into a tiny garden area that was about five square feet and then into the living room. The area was beautifully landscaped with exotic shrubs and flowers. It was refreshing every time you walked through the house.

A pastor in a nearby village presented us with the gift of a young rabbit. We decided that the perfect place to keep her would be our little enclosed garden. She loved her new home. It was fun to carry dinner to the table and watch our happy bunny frolicking in the tiny garden.

One bunny should have been enough, but then our night watchman suggested that we get a male rabbit in the market and raise baby bunnies. It sounded like a good idea, so for about two dollars we added a male to the enclosure.

Two or three mornings a week we had a traveling MK (missionary kid) preschool. We all took turns hosting it in our homes. It was my day to be hostess, so I had about five energetic preschoolers and toddlers running around the house. After our lesson they spied a large King lizard with a bright red head. They ecstatically began to chase it with sticks. They finally cornered it in the garden area. Just imagine five small, wild children waving sticks in a relatively small area and the two bunnies fearfully huddled in a far corner. Joel, a three-year-old hyperactive cherub, gave me a beatific smile and said, "See, Aunt Suzanne? We're helping the bunnies. They're so scared of the lizard." I guess it was all a matter of perspective.

Our bunnies began to multiply, and we were able to give rabbits to many of our pastors and neighbors. The diet here is often lacking in protein, so we were able to share the abundance God had given us. One day we were giving away a batch of bunnies, and four-year-old Sarah Joy put her foot down. "It isn't fair. The pastors eat bunny, the neighbors eat bunny, and I never get to eat bunny!" We quickly rectified that and cooked "bunny and dumplings" for dinner. I never could eat it. I know that the earth is the Lord's and he created everything for our enjoyment, but I just kept imagining that precious baby bunny that I had played with.

What about you? Do you have a hobby you enjoy that could be used to benefit others? We initially raised the bunnies for the pleasure of watching them and then were able to see them bless many people. If your hobby is sewing, you could make a dress for a premature baby or an orphan. If you're artistically inclined, you could sketch a pretty card to encourage a friend. If car repair or yard work is more your strength, you could help a single mother overwhelmed with those types of tasks. If you like to cook, you could make dinner for a new mom. The possibilities are endless to bless others with things that you enjoy doing.

Missionary Prayer Point: Pray for missionaries to be creative in the use of their talents to minister to others. Pray that even through their hobbies they would find avenues to give to others around them.

A God of Dreams

> But whatever was to my profit I now consider loss for the sake of Christ. What is more, I consider everything a loss compared to the surpassing greatness of knowing Jesus Christ my Lord, for whose sake I have lost all things. I consider them rubbish, that I may gain Christ and be found in him.
>
> Philippians 3:7–9

Maybe it shouldn't have been so important, but our video camera had become almost essential to me. Keep in mind that this was before email and digital cameras. Communication from the United States was steady but slow in coming. If I had a question, two weeks would pass before my letter got to my parents, and if they answered immediately, two more weeks would pass before I received the answer. I struggled with the idea that all of the grandparents were missing out on Sarah's and Rebekah's growing up. They were at that toddler stage where everything was new and cute. They were constantly developing new skills. John and I had been given a video camera before leaving the United States, and I frequently made videos of the girls and their adventures. Then I sent them to the grandparents, and it gave us all a real sense of connectedness.

One day I went to the closet to get the video camera but it was gone. I assumed John had used it and put it somewhere, but he denied having seen it. We searched and searched but could not find it anywhere. We finally realized that it had been stolen. It shouldn't have mattered so much, but I was really upset about it. We offered a reward and questioned employees but came up empty. I kept stewing about it. "God, I have come all this way to share you with these people. I don't ask much, but I want the grandparents to at least see their grandchildren growing up. Couldn't you give me that much?"

One month passed, then two months, and I was still angry about the missing video camera. Gradually God began to convict me about how much anger and emotional energy I was wasting over a material thing and how little concern I was showing over people's souls. I finally was able to release the whole situation to God and was really at peace about it.

During this time we had a part-time "gardener" who worked in our yard. He was a teenage boy who had approached us, needing money to pay his school fees. We had offered him some work on a weekly basis so he could meet his own needs. He had been working for us one or two afternoons a week after school doing yard work for quite some time. One morning he rang the doorbell and said, "Madame Missionary, promise me you won't send me to prison. I must talk to you." I gave him my word and he continued, "I stole your video camera. I saw it when you put it away, and I slipped in the back door and took it. Since that point in time your God has troubled me. I can't sleep and I can't eat. When I do sleep, he sends dreams to trouble me. Truly he is a powerful God. I want to return your camera and become a Christian."

That morning he prayed to receive Christ. He went home and returned the same day with our video camera. Surprisingly, it was none the worse for wear after its six-month sojourn in a hut.

God is a powerful God, and he can use anything to draw people to himself, even a video camera. Just be certain that you own your possessions instead of them owning you. Hold them loosely and be ready to use them for whatever God desires.

What about you? Are you angry over anything? Are you holding on to a sense of having been wronged? God is in control of you and your possessions. Release your anger to him and allow him to work in your situation. It may amaze you how God will work it out. He cares about even the small details in our lives, including our possessions and, more importantly, our attitude toward them. When the Israelites wandered in the wilderness, God prevented their shoes and clothes from wearing out—for forty years! If he can care for such a seemingly minor detail for the Israelites, then he can surely help you.

Missionary Prayer Point: Pray for missionaries to hold their possessions lightly and to keep life in perspective. Sometimes it is easy to get caught up with "stuff" and forget that the souls of people will endure forever.

The Wife Swap

> A happy heart makes the face cheerful. . . . The cheerful heart has a continual feast.
>
> Proverbs 15:13, 15

I have a good sense of humor and realize that God uses that to help me survive life overseas. I did not realize that God could use something that simple to help plant a church in Togo. John and I wanted to start a church on top of the mountain behind our house in the community of Soumdina Haut. In Togo, before you can begin work in a village, you must meet with the chief and ask his permission.

We were in the chief's compound. We were sitting on short stools inside a circle of thatched huts in the shade of a mango tree, surrounded by members of the chief's entourage who were curious about why we were there. We carefully greeted everyone, inquiring about their health, children, sleep, work, fields, and so forth. It would have been extremely rude to just come directly to the point. They had likewise inquired about us and offered us something to drink. Now with all the preliminaries taken care of, we were ready to make our proposal. We explained that we would like to come to their village on a weekly basis to do health teaching and to tell Bible stories in the hopes of one day establishing a church there.

The chief very solemnly considered our idea and then replied, "I can see you want to help our village through health teaching and teaching us about your God. That is a good thing, but to plant a church here you must do one thing: give me your wife." Now here was a situation that had not been covered in our mission classes at seminary. John, wanting to give a culturally appropriate answer, responded like this: "Chief, you know that I am a Christian and an American and am permitted to have only one wife. If I gave you my wife, who would cook my sauce?" (In this culture men can't cook, so either their mother or wife has to cook for them.) The chief very sagely nodded his head and said, "I see your point. I'll tell you what we'll do. I'll trade you this wife for yours." He pointed to his oldest, most toothless wife. I personally did not think it was a fair trade at all! We began to laugh, and the chief not only gave us permission to work in his village, but he also invited us to hold our meetings in his courtyard.

Later, he told us that many missionaries had trekked up his mountain for permission to start a church and had left feeling insulted and offended at his suggestion. Since we laughed and joked with him, he granted us permission to work in his village. So you see, God can use even a sense of humor to accomplish much for his kingdom.

What about you? Are you dealing with a difficult or uncomfortable situation at work or at home? Try to find the humor in the situation. There is usually something funny in even the most difficult situations if we will look for it. It won't take the problem away, but looking for laughter during the difficult times can make your load easier to carry.

Missionary Prayer Point: Pray for missionaries to maintain their sense of humor and to be able to laugh at the day-to-day absurdities that they encounter.

Stop, Thief!

> Then Peter came to Jesus and asked, "Lord, how many times shall I forgive my brother when he sins against me? Up to seven times?" Jesus answered, "I tell you, not seven times, but seventy-seven times."
>
> Matthew 18:21–22

I was in the kitchen cooking dinner, impervious to the visitor in my living room. A beggar had come into the courtyard of our house, and seeing no one around, he entered the living room. There he proceeded to slip John's radio into his pocket and make his exit. Fortunately, as he left he bumped into John and the radio fell out of his pocket. John recognized it, claimed it, and confronted the man. He promptly sat down on our porch and said, "I'm handicapped and can't walk well, so I'm not leaving until you give me cab fare." For a thief, he was certainly brazen.

In another incident, this same man approached another missionary for financial help. When he was turned down, he acted offended. He said, "Fine, I'm leaving!" He grabbed a backpack by his feet and marched out of the gate. About the time he got out of the gate, the missionary realized the man had just carried away her son's backpack with all his school books. What followed was a Keystone Cops chase with the missionary and her son in their truck chasing a handicapped thief on the back of a motorcycle. They finally managed to get the books back.

A few years passed, and I was running a clinic at the prison. I looked up and realized that my next patient was this same thief who had repeatedly stolen from all the missionaries. How would I respond? There was only one thing to do: I tried to meet his needs with kindness and compassion. Christ chose to forgive us of our many sins. We therefore must pray, "Forgive us our sins as we forgive those who have sinned against us."

What about you? Do you harbor bitterness or anger over a wrong committed against you? Reread the story of the unforgiving servant in Matthew 18:21–35. We were forgiven a great debt when God saved us from our sins. We have no choice but to freely offer forgiveness to those who have wronged us.

Missionary Prayer Point: Missionaries are often harassed and taken advantage of. Pray for them to be gracious and patient in dealing with difficult people. Pray that they would have a forgiving spirit toward those who wrong them.

Neighborliness

> Do not forsake your friend and the friend of your father, and do not go to your brother's house when disaster strikes you—better a neighbor nearby than a brother far away.
>
> Proverbs 27:10

We had been settled in our three-bedroom duplex for a couple months when an opportunity presented itself to us. Some missionary friends were returning from furlough and moving into a new home about an hour from us. Unfortunately, when they got to Kara, they found that their house was not finished yet. So we did the only natural thing: we invited them to stay with us until their house was completed.

Things were a bit snug because we had two two-year-olds and the Colemans had two teenagers, but the eight of us soon settled into a fairly comfortable routine. One point of conflict, however, was the sleeping arrangements. The two teenagers slept in the living room, and like most American teens, summer for them meant a chance to sleep late. My two-year-olds didn't believe in sleeping late, so we had to instigate new rules. "No touching Jacob and Rebekah until they're awake" was one rule that apparently wasn't explicit enough. The next morning a sleeping teen moaned, "Mom, they're breathing on me!" We looked up to see Sarah and Bekah standing about six inches from the sleeping form of a teen with their hands carefully tucked behind their backs. They were definitely obeying the letter of the law because they weren't touching them.

We also managed to start quite a few rumors in the marketplace. Gaye Coleman and I would go shopping together and plan our meals as we saw what was available. "Don't get a cabbage; I already have one," I might call out, and so forth. It became obvious we were shopping for the same household, so the market ladies drew the only logical conclusion: we must both be the wives of the same man. We quickly corrected that misconception, but I don't know if they ever did believe me. It was amazing how much I learned from Gaye about cooking in Africa in the weeks they spent with us.

We definitely had some tense moments, as is inevitable in the blending of two very different households, but the end result of the six weeks we lived together was a truly intimate friendship. It has survived ten years and several moves and has been a source of much comfort to me in some very difficult times. In seeking to give, I received abundantly more than I ever could have imagined. Gaye and I still laugh as we remember two little girls calling out every night, "Good night, Jacob," "Good night, Rebekah," and so forth until everyone had been appropriately spoken to and had reciprocated the good night. Truly when we share of ourselves we receive infinitely more in return.

What about you? Do you give of yourself freely to your friends? Even if it means some inconvenience to you, seek to minister to your friends. Don't give a thought as to what you will get back. Be hospitable! The rewards are unimaginable.

Missionary Prayer Point: Pray for missionaries to develop truly intimate friendships that will help carry them through difficult times. Pray that they would be willing to be hospitable and open to others around them.

Mentoring

> And the things you have heard me say in the presence of many witnesses entrust to reliable men who will also be qualified to teach others.
>
> 2 Timothy 2:2

We made it a habit to introduce ourselves to any Americans we happened to see in town. We would usually invite them over to our house and try to help them in any way we could. We had certainly been on the receiving end of help often enough when we were settling in and wanted to return the favor.

One time we met a team of about a dozen college students who were in town exploring the possibility of becoming missionaries after they finished school. They were young and enthusiastic. Just being around them was like a breath of fresh air as we viewed through their eyes things that had become commonplace to us. We took them with us to various villages and showed them how we went about planting churches. We answered a million questions and tried to give them a realistic picture of what life was like for a missionary in Togo.

After a few weeks of staying at a Togolese motel and eating local food, the young people were longing for a taste of home. We invited them over for brownies, ice cream, and a movie. They thoroughly enjoyed themselves. A little taste of America can go a long way toward easing culture shock!

Later one of the team members became very ill, so the group brought him to us for help. He had malaria and was running a high fever. They did not feel that they could adequately take care of him at the motel. We got him settled into our guest room, began rehydrating him, and offered him some malaria medication. I explained all the side effects and that there had been complications and even deaths in people with a previous history of heart problems. I also told him it was the treatment that we took and gave to our children. He agreed that it sounded like the best option and swallowed the pills.

Meanwhile, John had been trying to call the team's director to see what he wanted us to do for the young man. He finally got the director on the phone, took a message, and yelled to us, "Suzanne, he said to go ahead and treat him, but whatever you do, don't give him Halfan. A bunch of missionaries have died from it!" My patient's eyes grew as big as saucers—that was exactly the medicine he had taken about thirty minutes earlier at my recommendation. He already felt miserable with malaria, but now my poor patient was firmly convinced that he would die far from home. He spent a very restless night, but he woke up the next morning very much alive and feeling a lot better. Now that I think about it, he was the last medical patient that particular group brought to me.

Mentoring is so important. It doesn't have to be a formal relationship. You can simply bring people with you wherever you go and show them how to do whatever it is they want to learn. Some of the young people in the group that had followed us around came back to Kara as missionaries a few years later. They have been here for over five years now, and guess what? Their church-planting methods strongly resemble ours, and they are some of the most hospitable missionaries that we know.

What about you? Are there any young people in your life that you are choosing to help and mentor? Maybe your children are grown and you could help a struggling younger mom. Your words of encouragement and example as she sees you interacting with her children could make a world of difference for her and her family. Maybe you have been teaching Sunday school for years and could ask someone to be your assistant. As you work together, you can teach him or her what has worked for you, and soon the church will have another trained and eager teacher who is equipped to lead. It is essential that we deliberately mentor young people if the church is to grow.

Missionary Prayer Point: Pray that experienced missionaries would be eager to mentor younger missionaries and help them learn to function well in their locale. Pray that new missionaries would have a teachable spirit and would actively seek out a mentor.

Part 3

Return to Togo as Career Missionaries

(1997–2000)

My Husband's Funeral

> Finally, brothers, whatever is true, whatever is noble, whatever is right . . . whatever is admirable—if anything is excellent or praiseworthy—think about such things. . . . And the God of peace will be with you.
>
> Philippians 4:8–9

I have been gifted—or cursed (depending on your perspective)—with an extremely vivid imagination. Unfortunately, I can sometimes let it run away with me to the detriment of those around me.

John and I had served for two years with the IMB (International Mission Board) as International Service Corps volunteers and now wanted to become career missionaries. This process involved many interviews and many exams both psychological and physical. We were in Atlanta waiting on all the tests to come back. Late one evening while John was at work, I realized that I had not checked the mail all day, so I walked down to the mailbox and found a letter from Virginia. I opened it up and discovered I had passed my physical. Unfortunately, John had not. The letter went on to discuss a shadow in his lungs and a blood test that was way out of kilter. I couldn't contact John on the phone because by that time he was in rush-hour traffic, so I called a friend who was a physician. He told me there were several possibilities for the shadow, including lung cancer, tuberculosis, or simple scarring. The blood work might indicate acute leukemia, but he would need to do some more testing. He told me to send John to the office Monday morning.

As soon as I hung up the phone I began to cry. I was certain that I was soon going to be a widow. I really let my imagination run amok. I planned the funeral and tried to figure out what I was going to do to support our three children (while we were in the USA applying to become career missionaries, we had been blessed with adopting a third child, Christopher). My reasonably healthy husband was a bit surprised to come home to a hysterically weeping wife who had already buried him.

It took weeks of testing to get to the bottom of it all. The shadow turned out to be simply that—a shadow. John had been standing slightly crooked for the original X-ray. And the blood work showed he had a fairly rare parasite he had picked up in Africa. Once the CDC found it, it was a matter of simply swallowing six pills and he was well. All of that energy had been wasted with fretting and worrying over things that never happened.

What about you? How often are you guilty of letting your imagination run wild and living in the "what if" mode? Do you waste time worrying about things that may never happen? Take Paul's advice to the Philippians and choose to dwell on things that are true, pure, lovely, and admirable. I especially struggle with dwelling on what is true. Instead of worrying about what might happen, live in the present and allow the Holy Spirit control over your thoughts.

Missionary Prayer Point: Missionaries live in a world where there are frequent coups, robberies, and strange illnesses. Pray that they would have wisdom to deal with each actual crisis they face and be able to put aside worry and fear about possibilities they may or may not face.

The Lord's Supper

> And when he had given thanks, he broke [the bread] and said, "This is my body, which is for you; do this in remembrance of me."
>
> 1 Corinthians 11:24

In our many years on the mission field, we have celebrated the Lord's Supper in several types of settings and in different ways. The first time I remember receiving the elements in Africa was at New Jerusalem Baptist Church. They set up small cups of Coke and a loaf of bread on a table, and believers were invited to come and partake. I was sitting in the women's section with my daughters. Before going forward I turned to three-year-old Sarah Joy and briefly explained that she had not yet reached the age of accountability and had not been baptized, so she was not to touch anything on the table when she went forward. She irrepressibly replied, "I can reach anything on that table, so I can reach 'countability too!" A glare from me convinced her she had better obey, and we went forward to celebrate the Lord's Supper.

One of the most meaningful celebrations occurred in the village of Koutougou. John had planted a church there, and we were planning to have a baptism the same day as the Lord's Supper. Imagine what it would be like not only to have never had the opportunity to celebrate the Lord's Supper, but to have never even seen it celebrated.

We drove for a couple hours through the bush. The grass was as tall as the car, and often we felt like we were wading through an ocean of grass. In some places we couldn't see anywhere except straight in front because the grass was so tall and thick. Then it would give way and we would see a yam field, a mud hut with a thatch roof, or maybe a few trees with brilliant tropical birds. It was a long, bumpy ride, and we had to cross several bridges. At one point the children and I had to walk over a bridge just in case it wouldn't hold the weight of the car. We finally arrived to find the schoolhouse where the schoolmaster graciously allowed us to hold church services on Sundays. The church members had even picked flowers to decorate the front of the church. We had a beautiful service, and the Christians joyfully partook of communion.

Afterward we went to a nearby stream where we baptized several new converts. When we returned to the church the believers asked us to have a seat. They had killed a chicken and prepared a meal for us. Every family tries to raise a few chickens as meat for special occasions. About once a month they might kill and eat a chicken, yet out of their poverty they had given this chicken to us. Humbled by their generosity of spirit, we enjoyed a meal and left for home. We arrived home a few hours later, weary but filled with joy.

What about you? Has celebrating the Lord's Supper become commonplace for you? We have been given a rare gift in this tangible reminder of our Lord's death and resurrection. Receive it with awe and a grateful spirit as you meditate on what Christ did for us.

Missionary Prayer Point: Pray that missionaries would be faithful not only to evangelize but also to teach new believers the importance and significance of church ordinances such as baptism and communion. Pray that they would never lose their sense of awe over the death and resurrection of Jesus Christ.

Cookie Battle

> Each man should give what he has decided in his heart to give, not reluctantly or under compulsion, for God loves a cheerful giver.
>
> 2 Corinthians 9:7

After arriving in Togo, as a parent I found something that truly irritated me. If my children were eating a cookie in a public place, adults would approach them and say, "Give me some of your cookie." Of course, my toddlers would immediately scream and snatch it back. I just did not understand why grown-ups took so much pleasure in teasing and tormenting little kids, especially my kids.

One day I finally began to observe this scenario being played out with other people's children instead of just steaming about the wrongness of it. I noticed that a woman would approach another woman with a little baby who was holding something and ask him to give her some. She would gently pull the baby's hand toward her as if the baby was offering it to her, then release it and say, "Oh, you are such a kind baby. Thank you for sharing. I really don't want any." This culture highly values sharing and the giving of gifts and deliberately teaches it to children at an early age.

I would repeatedly see examples of this giving spirit during my time in Togo. If I gave a cookie to a three-year-old, he wouldn't stuff it into his mouth. Instead he would carefully break it into little pieces to be sure everyone got a taste. Whenever we go to a village to meet with a chief, we are always offered a gourd full of water, homemade beer, or palm wine. In some of these villages women have to walk for miles with a basin on their heads to draw water from a well or river. Yet when we drive up in our vehicle, they freely offer it to us.

I cannot begin to count the number of chickens and guinea fowl given to us through the years. When our son Benjamin was born, our neighbors came with a gift of a chicken and a big bag of fresh ginger "to be sure you make enough milk for the baby." Over and over I have been touched by the extreme generosity of the people we serve. Keep in mind that in Togo, the per capita income is only a little over four hundred dollars a year. Most people are struggling to survive, yet they give generously to strangers.

I must confess that I personally have struggled with being generous and at times react like my children, clutching my possessions and saying, "That's mine!" Some of the requests we receive are ludicrous: "Will you take off your dress and give it to me?" "Give me your daughter in marriage." "Give me a ticket to America." I usually just laugh at those requests. Other requests will always draw a yes response. If someone tells me he is hungry, I will always find food for him. It is very difficult at times to live in a place where poverty is so extreme and your means are limited. You sometimes have to make difficult choices. Yet I can look at my neighbors and be inspired by their generosity of spirit. Christ was ruler over the universe, yet he withheld nothing. He even gave his life for me. How can we choose to do otherwise?

What about you? Do you live your life with an open hand or a closed fist? God has promised us that if we sow generously we will also reap generously. Try today to find some way to share with someone in need.

Missionary Prayer Point: Pray that missionaries would not grow discouraged by all the needs that surround them. Pray that they would have generous hearts and discernment to know which needs to meet and how to meet them.

Pig in a Taxi

> She is like the merchant ships, bringing her food from afar. She gets up while it is still dark; she provides food for her family.
>
> Proverbs 31:14–15

Preparing delicious, nutritious meals from locally available ingredients has always been a challenge in Africa. Someone gave me a recipe for making ham and I was eager to try it. Of course, the first ingredient I needed was pork, and there was plenty of that running around town on the hoof. We made arrangements to purchase a pig for about twenty dollars from a nearby village. Naturally, we didn't want to haul that pig in our car, so for an additional dollar a bush taxi would pick him up and deliver him to our doorstep.

I went through my checklist to be sure I had everything I needed before the pig was delivered. I had buckets and salt to soak the meat in. The only ingredient I was missing was saltpeter. I couldn't find it in the French-English dictionary, but I knew it was a powder that was used in making gunpowder. I had also been told that it was available in our city market, so off I went.

Our market is huge. There is a two-story building in the middle, and for a whole city block vendors set up tables either in the building or under the shade of umbrellas and sell a bewildering assortment of merchandise. I felt I could pretty safely assume that the fish and vegetable ladies would not be selling my powder, so that ruled out a good portion of the market.

I walked over to the more exotic side of the market where the tables were covered with an interesting array of merchandise. There were dried chameleons and bats, assorted roots and herbs, and many different rocks and shells. All in all, it was amazing what these men had for sale.

I began going from table to table, explaining that I was looking for a powder that made gunpowder go *boom*. Gunpowder and private ownership of guns is forbidden, so you can imagine the looks I got from these men. Finally I heard someone call, "Psst—over here!" A man in a long veil and turban was secretively motioning me to follow him behind a curtained-off, private area. When I obeyed, he looked around to make sure we weren't being observed and opened a can of black powder. He told me, "Madame, if you sprinkle this on a fire you will get plenty of *boom*!" It appeared to be homemade gunpowder, and unfortunately, I needed only saltpeter, not actual gunpowder. I left the market empty-handed but undeterred in my ham-making experiment.

Early the next morning our pig was delivered to our doorstep with its feet tied together. Our guard killed it and the "fun" began. I had never realized how much of a pig is guts and skin! I was in the kitchen working on the meat as the guard cut it up and brought it to me. It was hot, tedious work. All of a sudden I heard Rebekah ecstatically call out, "Mama, come quick! The eagles came to see our piggy!" I went outside to find a row of vultures perched on our wall patiently waiting on us to finish cleaning our pig. After I had duly admired the "eagles," I went back to work.

It took most of the day, but by nightfall we had ham, ribs, sausage, pork roast, and so forth safely stashed in the freezer. Since I didn't have any saltpeter, my ham wasn't a pretty pink, but it tasted good. It was hard work but well worth the effort.

What about you? Are you willing to go the extra mile to prepare an enjoyable meal for your family? Try a new recipe this week and enjoy it with your family or a friend.

Missionary Prayer Point: Pray that missionaries would be creative in preparing delicious, nutritious meals for themselves and their families. Pray that they would use wisdom in their food choices and enjoy good health through healthy eating choices.

Of Hippos and Snakes

> Children, obey your parents in everything, for this pleases the Lord.
>
> Colossians 3:20

To vacation in Togo you have to get creative. For a time our family liked to get away to an old dam construction site. In the seventies the Germans very efficiently built living quarters for all the workers who came to build a huge hydroelectric plant. It was laid out like a regular suburb with cul-de-sacs, smooth paved roads, and even a recreation area with a pool. Some enterprising individuals purchased the property when the Germans finished the project, and they turned it into a hotel. They kept about ten of the bungalows in repair along with the pool and tennis courts.

The site was located in the middle of nowhere, so we had peace and quiet with no phones. It had electricity since it was connected to the dam project, and each bungalow came with four window air-conditioning units, a hot-water heater, and an electric stove. Electricity in abundance was a definite draw.

The area was also very beautiful. It was green and lush all year round, and there was a large population of hippopotamuses in the river that you could observe along with monitor lizards (very large lizards that look like small dragons), crocodiles, and other wildlife. The major drawback was that you had to carry everything you would need for your stay—sheets, dishes, pots, drinking water, food, and so forth, so you were limited in how long you could stay. We always looked like we were moving in when we went down there.

One morning I was determined to see the hippos. Our son Christopher was a baby, so John and I took turns babysitting him and going out on adventures. This morning John kept Christopher, and I had driven our four-wheel-drive vehicle as close to the river as I dared. Then the girls and I got out and hiked.

Before long the grass began to get deeper and to reach over our heads. The trail got narrower and the atmosphere just felt spooky to me, so I told the girls we were going to turn around. Sarah immediately asked, "Why?" I replied, "It looks really snaky to me. I don't think it's safe. We'll come back later when your dad can come with us." Sarah was not going to be deterred on her hippo hunt, so she held her head high and defiantly said, "There are no snakes out here, and I am not turning around." At that exact moment a snake slithered out of the grass across the path between the girls and right over Rebekah's feet. Needless to say, the girls immediately turned around and followed me back to the car.

I'm afraid that all too often I'm like Sarah. I read God's very clear directions in the Bible, but sometimes I'm tempted to say things like, "That's too hard." "No one really does that." "Surely he doesn't mean me." Or even, "I won't. I simply won't do that." Fortunately, we have a loving Father who doesn't allow us to disobey without consequences. He lovingly corrects us and leads us back into the direction he has for us. Sometimes the correction is as immediate and direct as Sarah and the snake; other times it is through a lack of peace and a gradual change in direction.

What about you? How do you choose to respond to God's Word? When you read his directives, do you rationalize your way out of obedience, or do you immediately do what he has ordered? It is only through obedience that you will find peace. Listen and obey God's directions. That is the way to peace and fulfillment.

Missionary Prayer Point: Pray for missionaries to be obedient in all areas of their lives. Pray that they would really seek God's face in every situation they encounter.

Fear in the Night

Keep me safe, O God, for in you I take refuge.

Psalm 16:1

Dark was falling and I was frightened. I wasn't just a little scared; I was deep-down scared. I had lived in Africa for some time and was accustomed to being home alone at night while John traveled, but this night was different. Lately the missionaries had been targeted in a series of late-night robberies. We had already been robbed once while John was home. It had been a very nonconfrontational robbery—we slept through it! I had gotten up to cook breakfast and found the kitchen door splintered and hanging on its hinges. The burglars had taken everything they could carry from the living room and kitchen while our night watchman apparently slept.

Then the robberies became more confrontational as the burglars began entering people's bedrooms instead of quietly slipping into the unoccupied rooms of the house. Just the night before I had been awakened at three a.m. by an American girl who needed medical help. She had been injured in a robbery at her house.

Now I was home alone and it was getting dark. Because of the frequent occurrence of robberies in unguarded homes, we have always had a night watchman, as do most other missionaries in this country. For the first time ever our night watchman had not shown up for work, and I was getting concerned. I fed the children their supper, locked up the house, and tried to maintain our usual bedtime routine.

Suddenly I heard a car horn at the gate. It was two dear missionary friends who had been caught by nightfall (we usually don't travel after dark here) and needed lodging for the night. Guess who was riding with them? My missing guard who had been attending a church conference with them! What had started out as a night of fear turned into a night of joy and laughter as my two friends and I set "burglar traps" on all the doors. You see, our house had not one or two but eight doors that all opened to the outside. We rigged up stools with cookie jars and bells and all sorts of noisemakers to let us know if anyone was coming in any of those doors. Then we got out magazines and proceeded to entertain each other with funny stories most of the night.

God was so faithful to keep me safe, and he gave me an entertaining evening with my friends to boot. There was no way those bells and cookie jars could have kept us safe from burglars, but just having friends there to share the adventure diminished the level of fear and made it more manageable. Their presence reminded me that God was with me and he would watch over me all through the night.

What about you? Do you sometimes let your fears grow out of proportion? Trust in God as your protector. He will watch over you, and he never sleeps.

Missionary Prayer Point: Pray for God's hand of protection on missionaries, especially in areas where they are frequently targeted by thieves and robbers. Pray that they would be courageous and not consumed by fear.

Rat Attack

> I will say of the Lord, "He is my refuge and my fortress, my God, in whom I trust." Surely he will save you from the fowler's snare and from the deadly pestilence.
>
> Psalm 91:2–3

Do rats count as a deadly pestilence? I think so, but I guess it depends on your perspective. John was traveling (somehow these things never seemed to happen when he was home), the children were tucked in their beds, and I was uneasily getting ready for bed. As soon as I turned out the light, I began to hear the wooden door leading to the garage shake. It sounded like someone was breaking into the house. I turned on the light and the racket stopped. I went through this routine several times with the night watchman reassuring me every time that there wasn't anyone there. I dozed off and then was suddenly awakened by the sound of shattering glass coming from my kitchen.

I tiptoed down the hall to investigate and walked into my kitchen to discover a nightmarish scene. Many plump, nasty rats were walking on my kitchen shelves pushing over glass bottles to get at the food inside of them. The noise I had heard earlier was the rats gnawing through the door. My first fear was that the rats might get in the bedrooms and harm the children. I promptly rousted my children out of their beds and moved them into my room at the far end of the house. I shut the door tight and went into the kitchen to do battle with my uninvited guests.

These brazen invaders had no fear. They did not even hide when I turned on the light! They sat on the shelves twitching their whiskers at me and then returned to their mayhem. I mixed up a tasty midnight snack of rat poison and peanut butter with a few dried sardines and left them to enjoy it. The next morning their dish was licked clean, and we had no more rat problems for a while.

I am truly afraid of mice and rats, but sometimes I have to go out and do battle. God will always give me strength for whatever battle I am facing at the moment, whether it is rats, a difficult child, or an illness.

What about you? What do you fear? Sometimes on behalf of others we have to do battle even with the thing we fear most. Live your life courageously instead of cowering in fear from whatever it is that you dread. God's grace is always sufficient, and we never face any trial alone.

Missionary Prayer Point: Missionaries often live far from any pest-control workers. Pray that they would be able to deal with the pests in their lives and would not be overwhelmed by them.

Super Kitty

> For by the grace given me I say to every one of you: Do not think of yourself more highly than you ought, but rather think of yourself with sober judgment, in accordance with the measure of faith God has given you.
>
> Romans 12:3

After our rat attack I began to rethink my stand on no indoor pets. Sarah Joy had been begging for a cat for months, and she had a birthday approaching. Some friends had kittens they were giving away, so for her birthday Sarah was presented with a tawny, orange and white male kitten. John and I explained to her that it was a boy kitten and she could name it anything she desired. She promptly dubbed the kitten "Victoria." We were a bit surprised and explained once more that it was a boy kitten, to which she replied, "You never know, if I give him a girl name he might grow up and have babies."

That poor kitten had expectations that he was never going to be able to live up to, so I guess he just decided not to fulfill any of our hopes. I probably should have realized that fact the first time I found Victoria and a mouse peacefully sharing a meal out of the same dish. I was still convinced that he would grow into a great mouser. He obviously just needed a little encouragement.

One morning as I was having my quiet time, I spied a small mouse frolicking on my clean dishes. I caught Victoria and stuck him in the cupboard with the mouse and shut the door. There was much yowling and scrambling about, and then out jumped Victoria, leaving the mouse to continue gallivanting on my dishes.

Victoria also delighted in tormenting visitors to our home. We have a wicker couch with movable cushions. Naturally, there is a small gap between the cushions. When a friend would sit on the couch, Victoria would crawl beneath the couch and begin poking them with his claw through the hole. They would look to see what they were sitting on and he would act as if he were asleep. It took us a little while to realize why our guests were so wiggly and uncomfortable on our couch.

Eventually Sarah caved in to the pressure and changed Victoria's name to Tiger, but he never did become a great mouser—or a mother.

What about you? Do you ever place unrealistic expectations on your children or others around you like Sarah did with her kitten? If people feel they can never measure up to your expectations, they may give up even trying. Look at yourself and others realistically. Do set high goals and expectations, but make sure you are not requiring the impossible.

Missionary Prayer Point: Pray that missionaries would not think of themselves "more highly than [they] ought" (Rom. 12:3), but that they would have realistic expectations of what they can accomplish.

Drama and a New Church

> That same day Jesus went out of the house and sat by the lake. . . . Then he told them many things in parables.
>
> Matthew 13:1, 3

We have found that the best way to plant churches in Togo is through telling Bible stories. The most important information is passed down from generation to generation through stories and songs. A majority of the population can't read, so "Chronological Bible Storying," which is simply telling stories that show God's plan for mankind's salvation, starting with Genesis and going through the entire Bible, is a wonderful way to communicate the gospel. It gives illiterate people an oral Bible as they learn the stories and retell them.

When we returned to Kara in 1996, the chief from Abide's village paid us a visit. To be honest, my heart sank when I saw him. I thought he had come to demand that we return Abide to him or to express his discontent with her living situation. Instead he told us that through our care of Abide, he had seen love demonstrated toward his village, and he wanted his people to understand what we believed. At his invitation we began going to his village on a weekly basis to tell Bible stories. We would meet in his courtyard under a huge, very shady baobab tree. John would tell stories to the adults and I would teach the children. All in all, it was going well, but something was missing. There just didn't seem to be much enthusiasm among the listeners.

We decided that the next time we went out we would ask the people to act out the story after we told it. The story that week was on Moses killing the Egyptian and then fleeing to the desert. This time we definitely had plenty of enthusiasm. The villagers began to scour the fields and courtyards looking for various props they deemed necessary and acted out the story exquisitely. "Moses," with a knife quickly carved from a bit of wood, very enthusiastically murdered the Egyptian who was beating the Israelites with a whip made from a millet stalk. He then physically dragged the Egyptian across the courtyard and hid him under some cornstalks. It was very dramatic and very accurately depicted the story we had just told. Hodalo, a young African widow, was sitting next to me, and as she saw the story unfolding her face lit up. She turned to me and said, "Now I understand! I didn't get it before."

Sometimes we have to be innovative and willing to try new things. Christ certainly communicated his message in many different formats to many different types of people. We need to be willing to make the effort to communicate the gospel in creative ways to reach our audience, whoever they may be.

What about you? Are you passing down stories of how God has worked in your life to your children or other family members? Don't let this important part of your spiritual heritage get lost in the busyness of day-to-day life.

Missionary Prayer Point: Pray for missionaries to be open to new and creative ways to share the gospel. Pray that they would expend the effort and energy necessary to make the gospel appealing and understandable to their audience, whether they are in the jungles of Africa or an uptown apartment in Paris.

Courtyard Baths and Other Village Adventures

> Jesus replied, "Foxes have holes and birds of the air have nests, but the Son of Man has no place to lay his head."
>
> Luke 9:58

Koudjoukadaa was located about an hour from our home. A lot of people didn't get home from the fields until dusk, and we normally had to leave long before that time to get home before dark. John and I felt that if we were to start occasionally sleeping in the village, it would give us an opportunity to get to know people more intimately and have more of an impact on the village.

For the grand sum of four dollars per month, our family rented a few rooms in a village compound. Most homes here are laid out very differently from the typical American home. Most American homes have one roof with many rooms underneath it, and maybe a fence or a wall around the yard. In a Kabiye village compound, there are an assortment of rooms built as separate round huts or square buildings joined together by a wall with the courtyard in the middle. The kitchen is a freestanding building, the husband has his own building, each wife has her room that is a separate building, and so forth. Most of life happens in the middle of the courtyard, where there is usually either a shade tree or a thatch shade structure, since the small huts are simply too dark, hot, and small for staying in for any period of time. The courtyard is where the occupants prepare food to cook, visit, wash dishes, and so forth. Even though there is a kitchen where most of the actual cooking takes place, the preparation of the food occurs outdoors.

The courtyard is definitely the place to be if you want to get to know people. Hodalo was a recent widow, and her deceased husband's rooms in the compound were vacant. It was a perfect solution for both of us. It gave her some needed cash and gave us a chance to really be a part of the village. Typically each compound in the village is located anywhere from fifty yards to half a mile from the next compound, and each one is surrounded by fields.

Our time in Koudjoukadaa definitely provided many lessons in cultural adaptation for us and much laughter for the villagers, who could not believe we had survived into adulthood with such poor skills. The first time I tried building a cooking fire, it kept going out. The women all tsk-tsked, had a good laugh, and then built a fire for me in about two minutes.

Another sore spot for me was the shower stall. Privacy concepts are very diverse in different cultures. The shower stall was located in the middle of the compound so a person could talk to everyone while bathing. Unfortunately, the walls only came to just above my waist if I was standing. To the amusement of everyone I would haul my bucket of water to the shower stall and squat down like a crab, trying to wash without landing in the mud. My girls were supposed to guard the entryway, but they just stood there and collapsed in gales of laughter at my contortions. I'm afraid the rest of the compound found me unfriendly, but I never did master the art of bathing and carrying on a conversation at the same time.

Another night John went outside to do his business and didn't realize he was standing on a line of army ants until they swarmed up his leg and made their presence known. We were definitely out of our comfort zone.

Yet it was worth all the discomfort the day we held our first baptism at Koudjoukadaa. In spite of persecution, six people stood up and were baptized. One eighty-year-old blind woman even leaped out of the baptismal waters and began to spontaneously dance and praise God.

What about you? Are you willing to move out of your comfort zone to share Christ with others? Take a risk. Go on a mission trip or simply share Christ with people who are different from you. Christ certainly moved out of his comfort zone. He went from having heaven itself as his home to not having anywhere to lay his head. We need to be willing to follow his example.

Missionary Prayer Point: Pray for missionaries to be willing to take risks and step out of their usual routine to share Christ with others.

Viper Bite

> Shadrach, Meshach and Abednego replied to the king, "O Nebuchadnezzar, we do not need to defend ourselves before you in this matter. If we are thrown into the blazing furnace, the God we serve is able to save us from it, and he will rescue us from your hand, O king. But even if he does not, we want you to know, O king, that we will not serve your gods or worship the image of gold you have set up."
>
> Daniel 3:16–18

Pocona was a man small in stature but big in faith. He was the only Christian leader in a vast area. A father of seven children, he was well respected in his community in spite of his faith. One evening when we stopped by his house, he told us he had been bitten by a viper, a very poisonous snake, the night before. We immediately offered to carry him into town to seek medical care. However, he had already sent someone into town and found out the hospital didn't have any antivenin in stock. He decided that he would prefer to remain at home with his family.

His leg continued to swell, and he began to have trouble breathing. He was very frightened. The local witch doctor paid him a visit. "You know this wouldn't have happened if you hadn't angered the spirits by turning away from them. I have access to snakebite medicine. All you have to do is offer one sacrifice to the spirits," he seductively propositioned.

"No!" Pocona replied. "I would rather die in the hands of God than live in the hands of Satan." With that courageous proclamation he sent the charlatan on his way.

The next few days were difficult for all of us. We finally located a hospital many hours away that had a few doses of antivenin, but the staff wouldn't sell it to us. "It's too late to do any good. The medicine won't help, and we have to save it for someone who can be saved."

We prayed fervently, but the poison continued its unremitting spread throughout his body. He was in agony, but all we were able to give him was ibuprofen and Benadryl. He told us one night he felt the swelling rise and completely cut off his respiration. He knew he was dying. Then miraculously the swelling diminished and he began to breathe again. From that point on he gradually improved, the swelling continued to diminish, and his good health was restored. No one in his village could believe he had survived. His testimony to the power of God drew many people to the Lord, and his church grew. The people in the community were amazed that the spirits did not seek retribution on him for turning away the witch doctor. They began to see that God was more powerful than the spirits. One day a few weeks later, we drove up to find that five-feet-five-inch-tall Pocona had killed a twenty-foot-long water snake and invited the village to come feast on the grilled snake. He may have been small in stature, but his courage and righteousness became known for a great distance.

What about you? Your stand for Christ probably won't cost you access to medicine that you need, but it may cost you in some way. Are you willing to take a stand for what is right at home, at work, and at play? People are watching you as a Christian, just as they watched Pocona. They want to see if Christ really makes a difference in your life. Live courageously!

Missionary Prayer Point: Pray that missionaries would have wisdom in discipling new believers. Pray that the new believers would completely reject idols and turn wholeheartedly to Christ to meet all of their needs.

Elephants and Yams

> Jesus replied, "They do not need to go away. You give them something to eat."
>
> Matthew 14:16

Most people in Togo are subsistence farmers. When you read that information in a book, it seems like a plain, dull fact. Yet the reality is quite different. Being a farmer means that all most people have to eat is what they are able to grow. If a family has four children, they have to plant enough fields and grow enough food to feed the entire family until the harvest the next year. They usually do not even have farm animals, tractors, or plows, so they have to work with rudimentary hand tools like a short-handled hoe. The ground is hard and rocky and difficult to work. I once had a pastor's wife who was nine months pregnant tell me, "Please pray that I won't go into labor before we finish planting. Otherwise we won't have enough to eat this year." Everyone in the family helps. Even small children and the elderly poke holes in the mounds of dirt and carefully plant the seeds in the fields that younger backs have prepared.

There is not much margin for error. In good years people often have enough surplus to sell. They use the money to purchase "luxuries" like clothes and medicine, to pay school fees, or, sometimes in a really good year, to purchase a family bicycle for transportation. If there is not enough rain or too much rain, people starve the next year. Usually the children and the elderly suffer the most.

This year (1998) seemed to be a good year. The crops looked healthy alongside the road. The rain had come in the right amounts and at the right time. It wasn't much longer until harvest. Everyone was jubilant and couldn't imagine that anything could go wrong at this late date.

When we stopped at Pastor Pocona's house, we noticed that he looked unusually haggard. "What's wrong?" we asked. He told us he had been up all night in his yam fields tending a fire and beating a drum, trying to scare away the small herd of elephants that live in Togo. No one is allowed to harm or to harass the elephants. They are well protected by the government, which is as it should be. Unfortunately, the elephants had moved into the vicinity of Bebeda, a village in Togo, and were finding the yam fields irresistible. They would come in at night, wrap their trunks around the vines, and uproot the baby yams. What they didn't eat they smashed and trampled underfoot. People were starting smudge fires and beating drums all night long in hopes of scaring the elephants away. Yet the elephants continued their feeding spree, oblivious to the damage they were causing.

The villagers sent a delegation into town to ask the government for help. The army "buzzed" the elephants with helicopters, hoping to scare them away from the cultivated areas. The elephants fled, but by nightfall they were back. By the time the crops were ripe enough to be harvested, the elephants had devastated the fields of about one hundred farmers.

You can imagine the heaviness of heart as people salvaged what they could of their crops. The rains would not begin for another six to eight months. The people knew that this year there would be a good deal of famine in their village. We had watched and prayed alongside these villagers. We knew they had done everything humanly possible, but they still had not succeeded with their crops for this year.

Fortunately, many Americans give to the Hunger Relief Fund of the IMB. For less than five thousand dollars, we were able to provide every family with over two hundred pounds of dried corn to see them through the season. The look of joy on people's faces as the truck arrived with the corn was indescribable. Now there would be enough food because someone in America had given money for hunger relief.

Oftentimes churches raise money for hunger-relief projects, but the members don't know where the money goes. I am here to tell you that the village of Bebeda received some of these funds, and it made a life-and-death difference for them.

What about you? Are you often cynical about hunger-relief projects? You may often feel bombarded by images and overwhelmed by the neediness of the rest of the world. Yet you can make a genuine difference by contributing to legitimate hunger-relief projects.

Missionary Prayer Point: Pray that missionaries would not shun relief projects because of feeling overwhelmed by the needs and the amount of work required. Pray that they would be wise stewards of the funds available to them and that they would be able to feed the hungry as the need arises.

Toilet Paper Wedding

> The Spirit and the bride say, "Come!" And let him who hears say, "Come!" Whoever is thirsty, let him come; and whoever wishes, let him take the free gift of the water of life.
>
> Revelation 22:17

I knew that our family was not at an American wedding when we showed up at the time indicated on the invitation and found an empty church. I guess I should say "almost empty" because the wedding DJ was there and ready to begin his work of keeping the wedding animated. He immediately began his patter: "Here come the Americans—everyone applaud!" Since we were the only ones there, he didn't manage to raise much applause, but he kept right on talking, completely unfazed.

We found our seats and I began to look around. Almost all the decorations were made of pink toilet paper. There were pink flowers and pink streamers from the toilet paper. The wedding car just outside the church was very carefully decorated with cotton balls and more pink toilet paper stuck on with dots of condensed milk. I began to wonder just how much toilet paper I would see in this wedding.

People continued drifting in until the church was packed. The DJ made his big announcement: "The wedding party is here!" By that time it was well over one hundred degrees in the sanctuary, but the groom and his best man were dressed in wool suits with long-sleeved white shirts. They began dancing down the aisle—one step forward, side step, two small steps back. This was accompanied by music from cowbells, drums, and gourds covered with buttons. The DJ kept up his patter for the entire thirty-minute dance down the aisle.

Then it was time for the main event. First two little girls came up the aisle, wrapped in a long piece of handwoven fabric. Their faces and shoulders were painted with white dots. They began to dance and throw what looked like confetti from a basket in their hands. I later found out that it too was made from toilet paper and shiny rickrack that had been chopped into tiny bits. After they were partway down the aisle, the bride appeared at the back. The DJ made his announcement and the crowd went wild, cheering, clapping, and whistling their approval.

There is only one way to tell if a woman is going to be a hardworking wife: by how much of a sweat she works up coming down the aisle. Here was this woman beautifully arrayed in a long white gown, a veil, and high-heeled shoes, dancing for all she's worth—forward, side, back, back.

Over and over she repeated the pattern. The flower girls threw bits of toilet paper in the air, and it descended like a sparkling cloud on the bride as—forward, side, back, back—she continued her dance. She was dripping with sweat at that point, and her maid of honor stepped forward to do her job. She squirted perfume and deodorant all over the bride, who did not hesitate in her dance.

I watched in surprise as an older woman darted out of the crowd and lifted the bride's veil. She pressed a coin into the bride's forehead. If the bride was sweaty enough for it to stick, it was proof that she would be a hardworking wife. After a few more dance steps, the coin fell to the ground. Another member of the bridal party followed behind, collecting the coins in a basket as a gift for the bride. More members of the audience came forward, pressing their coins onto the bride's face, and every single one stuck. The DJ announced when each coin stuck, and the crowd shouted in approval.

Finally, after an hour of dancing, the bride arrived at the front of the church. She sat next to her groom on a wooden couch facing the audience. She was very careful not to smile. A smile would show that she was not serious about the marriage.

The couple was serenaded by a number of church choirs from many different denominations. After the singing there was a long message titled "The Christian Family." Then another pastor stood up to perform the actual ceremony. First he told the story of how Jacob was deceived into marrying Leah instead of Rachel. He told the groom that he did not want him to be deceived. He instructed the groom to lift the veil and verify that this truly was the woman he wanted to marry. The groom made a game of it. He very carefully rolled back the veil a few inches and tried to peek at his bride. A few more inches and a peek, a few more inches and he revealed his bride's face. He heaved a sigh as his face split into a huge grin. This was the only smile seen in the entire wedding.

The DJ actually hushed for a moment and handed the groom the microphone. The congregation held their breath as they waited for the groom's pronouncement. "Yes, this is the woman I want to marry!" he emphatically stated. The crowd cheered and the wedding ceremony continued.

After the pronouncement of man and wife, the gift giving began. One by one or in groups people danced forward with gifts for the couple. As I looked toward the back of the church, it appeared that a large metal basin and a mortar and pestle for making foufou were dancing themselves down the aisle. I looked again and realized they were traveling on the heads of the women presenting them as gifts. Down the aisle the dancers came, presenting the couple with everything they needed for setting up house. They would receive palm-frond fans for starting cooking fires, cauldrons for cooking, and basins and buckets for carrying water. On and on the gifts came.

By that time it was getting dark since the celebration had gone on all day. Two of our children were asleep under our bench. We decided to skip the reception and head home. At the reception there would be a full meal, much dancing, and celebrating until the wee hours of the morning. Christian weddings were a rarity and were considered a wonderful reason for a celebration.

What about you? The Bible tells us that one day our bridegroom, Christ, is coming for us. Are you ready for his coming? Have you been born again, and are you keeping your garments clean and white through regular confession of sin? Be prepared. We do not know when Christ will appear.

Missionary Prayer Point: Pray that missionaries will be able to clearly present God's plan for the family to their new converts. Pray for the new believers to be able to establish strong Christian homes in spite of the paganism that surrounds them.

Communication Challenges

> Before a word is on my tongue you know it completely, O LORD.
>
> Psalm 139:4

It is easy for me to get sidetracked in all the details of language learning and lose sight of the big picture. John is much better at learning how to actually communicate instead of getting hung up on all the intricacies of grammar in language.

"Do you realize there are thirty-six words for 'it' in Kabiye?" I raved one day. "Which 'it' you use depends on if the noun you refer to is masculine, feminine, or neuter and what tense it is in—past, present, future, sort of in the past, having happened a long time ago, happening a long time ago over a period of time, and so forth. In this crazy language, you conjugate the nouns!" My husband was not aware of this essential fact, but he was still out and about and communicating with people. He gently reminded me that it really didn't matter if I ever understood the grammar. The important thing was to be able to talk to people and understand them. He was exactly right.

I decided that the neighborhood children would make a good audience and asked my language assistant to help me organize a series of lessons. We looked like the Pied Piper and his assistant walking down the road, with about a hundred children following us to the church. None of the neighborhood kids had access to TV or many entertainment options, so we were the best thing going. I made homemade popsicles, we planned games and music, and, most importantly, we had a Bible story in Kabiye. Everyone benefited. The kids enjoyed the outing, and it gave me some much-needed practice in Kabiye instead of fretting over grammar.

During one of the lessons on the Old Testament prophecies fulfilled in Christ, a young girl popped out of her seat and said, "It's true! It's really true! Jesus really is the Messiah!" You have to understand that in most schools here there are over one hundred students per teacher. Students are beaten if they even think of speaking out during lessons, so it was extremely unusual for her to speak out in the middle of a story. She was just overwhelmed with excitement. She belonged to another religion that taught that Jesus was a good man but only human and not divine.

I was learning the language so that people like this little girl could hear the message of Christ. It really did not matter if I ever managed to conjugate the word "it" or not.

What about you? Do you ever lose your focus on what is truly important? Keep your mind fixed on Christ and on what he desires for you to accomplish daily. Don't get so bogged down in the details that you lose track of the big picture.

Missionary Prayer Point: Pray for missionaries to keep their focus on why they are on the mission field. Pray that they wouldn't get so bogged down in the details of day-to-day life that they forget why they came to the mission field.

Quandary

> Whoever welcomes a little child like this in my name welcomes me.
>
> Matthew 18:5

My heart sank as I answered the door and saw "T" standing there. (I'm not using her real name because she still could face persecution if her family knew of her faith in Christ.) She was the young girl who had popped out of her seat at the Bible study the previous week because she was so excited about discovering who Christ was. We knew her family had been beating her for associating with us. "Madame Missionary, can I come in?" she asked timidly. What a quandary—refuse to allow her inside to study the Bible and hope that her family would not realize she had knocked on our door so she could avoid another beating, or let her come in, knowing what would happen to her. There was no good choice.

She assured me that her mother had told her she could come to see me and her father was out of town, so I let her inside. It was Christmastime, so we sat down with the other girls who had come and enjoyed some Christmas cookies. I got out our manger scene and explained the Christmas story as I added each piece. They were enthralled because they had never seen a nativity set before.

It was not exactly a typical Christmas scene. We were sitting under a thatch apatam, similar to a gazebo, in the yard. We were enjoying cold drinks instead of hot ones since it was over one hundred degrees. There was a fine haze in the air from the Harmattan wind (a strong, dusty wind) blowing off the Sahara desert. All in all, the setting was about as different from a typical American Christmas as you can imagine, but the story was the same. Watching the wonder in T's eyes as she heard the story that was so new to her made me realize anew what Christmas is all about. She left our house that day excited and full of hope in a Savior who had come to earth as a helpless baby just for her.

Why do some people have to suffer so much for their faith while others almost take it for granted? I don't have the answer to that, but I do know that we have been given a precious gift in Christ and should treasure it.

What about you? How dear do you hold your faith? Realize what a gift we have been given to be able to openly believe and worship God. Treat your faith as the priceless treasure it is, and don't take your freedom for granted.

Missionary Prayer Point: Missionaries often work with people who are persecuted for putting their faith in Christ. Pray that they would be wise in their dealings with Christians and be strong even in the face of persecution. It is sometimes harder to watch those around you suffer for their faith than to suffer yourself.

Good Gifts

> Which of you, if his son asks for bread, will give him a stone? Or if he asks for a fish, will give him a snake? If you, then, though you are evil, know how to give good gifts to your children, how much more will your Father in heaven give good gifts to those who ask him!
>
> Matthew 7:9–11

Birthday parties. Just the mention of the word calls up all kinds of pictures to your mind, doesn't it? You think of cake, balloons, games, and lots of friends. Now, visualize a birthday party in Africa. What do you see? That is a bit more challenging to imagine, isn't it?

Being good American parents, we wanted our children's birthdays to be memorable. It takes just a bit of creativity to make it happen. One year the kids heard about piñatas. Nothing else would do. They desperately wanted a piñata. What is a loving parent to do except try to make it happen? I found directions for making one in a magazine. All I needed was a large balloon, flour and water paste, newspapers, and tempera paint.

Have you ever started on one of these "simple" projects that got more complicated as you went along? This project definitely fell into that category. First of all, I didn't have a large balloon, so I substituted a surgical glove. *Very creative of me*, I thought. Then came the fun part—we were to dip the strips of newsprint in the flour and water paste and drape them on the "balloon." Unfortunately, my balloon had fingers. I would very carefully tuck one finger in and lay a few strips over it, then I would do the next finger. About that time the first finger would come popping out, sending paste flying everywhere.

I had several assistants on this project. The number of assistants a person has will always compound the amount of time it takes to complete a project. My assistants were a toddler, a kindergartner, a first grader, and a dog, all of whom wanted to be sure they got to help. I don't know whether we or the piñata ended up being covered with the most paste.

We had only a couple of days until the party, but the piñata was supposed to dry in twenty-four hours, so I figured we were in good shape. Whoever wrote the magazine article was obviously not living in Africa during the rainy season. The next day the piñata was extremely soggy. I was feeling a bit of pressure now. The party was the next day, and my piñata was looking pretty sad. In small print the article mentioned that I could put the piñata in a warm oven to speed the drying process. I failed to read the even smaller print that mentioned popping the balloon before you lit the oven. I placed my piñata in the oven and went to work on another project.

A little later I heard a *boom!* from my kitchen. I came running to discover that my piñata had burst. Oh well, I needed a hole to put the candy in anyway. I didn't want to risk moisture from the paint making the piñata soggy again, so I very carefully covered it in wrapping paper and glue. Voilà! I had a piñata that smelled only slightly of burned rubber.

John felt strongly that we should have pony rides at the party, but there were no ponies available. He and another missionary went to the cattle yard and offered to rent one of the donkeys scheduled to be slaughtered. The owners were glad to make some money by delaying the butchering, so they agreed to bring the donkey to the house the next day.

The day of the party dawned bright and clear. The "pony," a very elderly donkey, stood patiently awaiting its moment in the spotlight. The piñata was filled with candy. The cake was decorated and the ice cream made. After our guests arrived, the fun began. We played traditional party games like Toss the Onion in the Calabash, balloon volleyball, ball-throwing contests, and so forth.

Then it was time for the two-pronged finale—the piñata and the donkey rides. There were fifteen children, and I was really hoping that each one would get a chance to swing at the piñata. One after the other they swung and swung. We went through the line three times and even got rid of the blindfold. The piñata was totally indestructible. When the fingers kept popping up, we realized we had put far too much papier-mâché on it. We finally just dumped out the candy and turned to our donkey ride.

We loaded the first child on and started to lead the donkey around the yard. The donkey would not budge. We offered it a carrot, but it had never seen a carrot before. Finally we had to resort to one missionary pulling the donkey and the other one pushing the donkey around the yard. After dragging the donkey around the yard fifteen times, the missionary dads were ready for some refreshments.

It may not have been a picture-perfect party, but the memories we built were priceless. My children knew they were loved and that their birthdays were important to us because they themselves were valuable. How much more valuable, then, are each of us to God, who desires to give us good gifts.

What about you? Do you realize that your heavenly Father has only good gifts for you? They may not be exactly what you think you want, but trust God—he truly does have your best interest at heart.

Missionary Prayer Point: Pray for missionaries to make memories with their families. Pray that they would be creative and would have meaningful celebrations to treasure for years to come.

The Orphan Ballet

> Religion that God our Father accepts as pure and faultless is this: to look after orphans and widows in their distress and to keep oneself from being polluted by the world.
>
> James 1:27

During our time in Togo and Benin we have tried to seek out orphans and help them in any way we can. In Togo, John discovered an orphanage right around the corner from our house. It was not a Christian orphanage or even a very well-managed one, and to us the condition of the children seemed deplorable. The director was a single man who liked to travel, so the children were without any supervision much of the time. The highest percentage of the children in the orphanage was teens and preteens with a very cynical outlook on life. There was rarely enough food, and most of the children had large running sores on their legs.

As we got to know the director, we realized he had a good heart but had taken on more than he could handle. He had become burdened about the "market children" he would see in town. These were children from about four years old to teenagers who were abandoned in the market. Sometimes their parents had died and the extended family was not willing to share food, or the parent was mentally ill and unable to care for the child. These children were simply left in the market to survive any way they could. They survived by begging, helping sell trinkets, carrying people's goods, or even stealing. They slept in the streets around the market at night.

The director had raised funds and rented a house and now had about forty children living with him. Their situation was now marginally better than it had been when they lived in the market. The government provided free tuition for them to attend school. They all had one or two sets of clothes, flip-flops, at least one meal a day, and, most importantly, a safe place to sleep.

We started dropping off staples like gunnysacks of rice and dried corn or truckloads of yams. Often the villages would give us bushels of peanuts during harvest time and we would give those to the orphanage as well. Gradually the children's diets began to improve, and the children themselves became healthier. We began to go to the orphanage every week to have a Bible study and bandage the children's legs. It was amazing how quickly the sores disappeared once we began bandaging and cleaning them regularly.

The children had often been mistreated and put down by others even in school since they were on the very bottom of the social ladder. They needed something at which they could succeed, so we gave them a weekly memory verse and worked with them until they all could recite it. Anyone who could recite it the following week would win a prize—an orange, bags of roasted peanuts, or sometimes candy. They all succeeded week after week.

We knew that the children had enjoyed very few celebrations in their lifetimes. We decided to have a feast at our house for them. We had to cook the main food outdoors over a fire because our stove was too small. A big holiday food in Togo is rice topped with spaghetti and served with a red sauce, so we borrowed a neighbor's cauldron and cooked fifty pounds of rice and fifteen pounds of spaghetti noodles. Aimee, our house helper, prepared several gallons of a meaty red sauce made from crushed sesame seeds, tomatoes, ginger, hot pepper, onions, and lots of oil.

It was time for our guests to arrive. I looked out the gate to see them arrive all cleaned up and dressed in the best they had. For once the neighborhood kids were looking at the orphanage kids with something akin to envy. We fed the kids—it was amazing how much food they were able to consume—gave them each a small gift, and showed them a movie. Since they didn't have access to TV, they thought that was a great treat.

At that point we thought the party was about over and started to say good-bye, but the orphans told us they had a surprise for us: they had prepared a ballet. *Ballet?!* I thought. They ran off into the backyard to change into their costumes. When they returned, they were arrayed not in pink tutus but in traditional handwoven clothes. The older boys played the drums, and what followed was unlike any ballet I had ever seen. They had been working on mastering some of the traditional Kabiye dances and rhythms. It was beautiful.

The children who did not dance acted out humorous skits they had written. We saw the world through their eyes as they performed slapstick skits of clumsy, evil police and smart simpletons who saved the day. We laughed until we cried. We were moved by the time and effort they had put into preparing this gift to us. Everyone finally wandered back home with their bellies full and a sense of contentment in their hearts.

What about you? In America today we meet few actual orphans, but the Bible often refers to orphans as "fatherless." I would venture to say that there are few of us who do not know any fatherless or motherless children. Single parents have an extremely difficult job. Why not see if there is anything you can do to lighten their load and care for the "fatherless" that you know?

Missionary Prayer Point: With the AIDS epidemic sweeping across Africa, Asia, and other parts of the world, missionaries are faced with many more orphans than ever before. At one orphanage we work with, the number of orphans has tripled in the last four years. Pray for missionaries to have wisdom, discernment, and compassion as they try to help these children and integrate them into society.

Typhoid and Malaria

> Praise the Lord, O my soul, and forget not all his benefits—who forgives all your sins and heals all your diseases.
>
> Psalm 103:2–3

My throat was on fire. It was painful to swallow. My fever shot up and I felt miserable. I decided to go ahead and take some antibiotics. After only a couple of days on antibiotics I became extremely nauseated and could not keep them down. Then my fever got even higher, and I really thought I was dying, so I took a malaria treatment. At that point John wanted to drive me to the doctor, but I was sure I would feel better and didn't want to face the seven-hour ride to medical care.

My fever eventually went down a bit, but then John began to run a fever. Now we were stuck because neither of us was well enough to drive. We both needed rest to recuperate, but there was a hitch in that plan: we had three very active children aged two, five, and six. We both felt terrible, but someone had to chase the children all day. We made a deal—whoever had the highest fever got to stay in bed. All day long we passed the thermometer back and forth and took turns caring for the children.

Fortunately, John responded rapidly to the malaria treatment and was feeling like himself in just a few days. But I just couldn't seem to shake the sickness. I kept running low-grade fevers and was incredibly weak and debilitated. I let things drag on like that for about six weeks, firmly convinced that after a little more rest I would feel better. Finally we made the seven-hour very hot and bumpy trek to the capital city. There I received a thorough tongue-lashing from the physician when my blood work was back. "You have typhoid fever. Don't you realize that you could have died?" Properly chastened, I took the correct medication and was feeling better in just a few days.

So often we try to take care of everyone else but fail to take care of ourselves. We think we are invincible. Sometimes by trying to do it all ourselves instead of accepting help, we can turn a minor problem into a major one. There is no shame in admitting we need help, and then getting it. Everyone needs help at some time.

What about you? Do you delay getting help when you need it? Sometimes it is hard to admit we need help physically, emotionally, or spiritually. Don't let things drag on for too long. Get the help you need promptly.

Missionary Prayer Point: Pray that missionaries would have access to medical care when they need it and the common sense to know when to get help. Pray for God's hand of protection over them as they face many diseases both common and exotic.

Premature Labor

> He asked Jesus, "And who is my neighbor?" . . . But a Samaritan, as he traveled, came where the man was; and when he saw him, he took pity on him.
>
> Luke 10:29, 33

The phone was ringing. It was the middle of the night. Oh no . . . it must be an emergency. I stumbled around in the dark until I found the living room phone. It was a missionary colleague asking for help. A friend of ours was in labor at only thirty-two weeks of pregnancy. If the baby came tonight, it might not survive, because we were too far away for the specialized care needed. It would take seven hours to drive to the city of Lome to see an obstetrician. Then, if the mother could get on a flight, it would take another seven hours of flight time to get to the closest NICU in Paris, France.

I didn't know exactly what I could do, but I was willing to help. I drove out into a very silent and dark town and was almost immediately stopped by soldiers who wanted to know what I was doing out past curfew. I showed them my medical bag and explained. After a number of questions they let me go on my way.

I arrived at my friend's house to find her having fairly regular contractions. Mike, a missionary who had been an EMT in America, was with her. We were very worried about the consequences of the baby coming this early. We immediately assessed the situation and began to pray. It soon became obvious that her contractions were not going to stop on their own with simply a little rehydration and rest.

An obstetrician in the United States had given Mike a kit of various medications and clear instructions on their use if he ever found himself in this situation. We started an IV and began to administer the various medicines. At this point our friend wasn't dilating any more, but her contractions weren't stopping either. We asked her husband to make arrangements for evacuation by plane, then continued to talk and pray with her and administer the medicine.

Mike and I were really getting worried because it looked like the baby was coming and we didn't have any life support equipment for it. I felt like Mammy in the movie *Gone with the Wind*, who said, "Miz Scarlett, I don't know nothin' 'bout birthin' no baby!" Mike and I would try to put on a calm and competent face in front of our patient and then quietly say to each other, "Can I speak with you in the hall?" We would go out in the hall and have a minor panic attack, then straighten our faces and walk back in the room to try to reassure our mom-to-be. We made a small baby warmer out of a trunk and hot water bottles. Mike had the equipment we needed to intubate the baby so we could manually help her breathe, but we had so little compared to what we needed.

I was thrilled to see the sun rise the next morning with the baby not yet born. As soon as it was daylight, a small plane landed and our friend was flown out to the capital city. She made it all the way to France where they continued her on the same drugs we had started in Togo. A month later their precious daughter, Michael, was born in Paris. God had been so good to save her life.

What about you? Do your neighbors know they can come to you for help? Maybe it can be as simple as keeping an eye out for their children playing outside or helping someone who can no longer drive to get groceries. Be willing to take the time to be a Good Samaritan.

Missionary Prayer Point: Pray that missionaries would be Good Samaritans, ready and willing to help those who approach them—even if it occasionally carries them out of their depth.

Death of a Friend

> Precious in the sight of the LORD is the death of his saints.
>
> Psalm 116:15

My friend Brigitte was dying. There was almost nothing left of her except a skeletal form and large, pleading eyes. She had always been a petite woman, but now she weighed only sixty pounds. Her mouth and throat were covered in sores. Eating, drinking, and even speaking had become agonizing. "Is there anything I can get for you? Anything I can do?" I asked as I visited her at the hospital. She whispered, "Batteries. Can you bring some more batteries?" Every day she asked the women from the church to continually play on a tape player a dramatized version of the New Testament in Kabiye. One of the other women in the hospital ward had already become a Christian through the tapes.

The stark hospital ward had nothing but utilitarian metal beds with rubber-covered mattresses. Patients were expected to bring their own sheets or some sort of cloth to cover the bed. They had to provide their own dishes and food. Flies buzzed everywhere, and the stench was horrendous. Beside each bed was a rickety metal IV pole with a glass bottle hanging from it. It was hot and crowded since each patient had family members staying with them to prepare the meals and bring water. In the midst of all this, what did my friend want? Batteries so that others could hear the Bible and be comforted.

Who was my friend Brigitte? She was a beautiful woman who had blatantly defied tradition by fleeing from an arranged marriage and instead marrying for love. This caused a deep rift with her family, who had already received the bride price and had to return it to the disgruntled suitor. She and her new husband lived in secret until she was pregnant. Up to that point her family could have forcibly married her to the older man who had paid the price for her. She was a lone Christian in a family that worshiped idols and ancestral spirits. When her husband, Komi, decided to move to Kara to help begin a new church, she gladly moved away from the conflict with her family.

Komi and Brigitte worked with a missionary beginning a church from scratch. The church grew and thrived. At the time I first met Brigitte, the church had almost four hundred regular attendees in an area where very few churches have more than fifty people in attendance. Brigitte was a seamstress and very active in church work, a dynamite woman with a ready laugh. She and her husband were some of the first visitors at our home in Kara. We counted them both as dear friends.

Then tragedy struck. First her husband died a painful, lingering death. Brigitte was already experiencing many symptoms of the same illness and knew she would not live long. Their two young daughters bravely tried to continue with their schoolwork, not really understanding what was happening.

My friend died as she had lived, trying to meet the needs of others around her.

After Brigitte's death, it was assumed that the children would go live with their grandparents as tradition dictated. It seemed unfair that these two girls who had been raised in a progressive Christian home would be turned over to a pagan traditional home to be married off at an early age.

Then there was a surprise announcement—the pastor and his wife had left a will. The will explicitly gave the care of their children to the church. Two of the deacons carried the girls home with them, paid their school fees so they could continue their education, and continued raising them according to their parents' values. A few years later, the extended family overturned the will and gained custody of the girls, but by that point the girls had enjoyed three more years of education in a Christian home.

Every once in a while the girls are allowed to visit. They have grown into beautiful, gracious young women who are mirror images of their mother. Eventually the extended family was shamed into doing what was right for them. They both have been allowed to continue their schooling, and even the sixteen-year-old has not been married off yet. Pastor and Madame Komi have lived on in the legacy of their daughters.

What about you? I was amazed at the death my friend died. In spite of extreme pain and hardship she died at peace, without any bitterness or rancor. How prepared are you to face death? Does anyone have anything against you? Are you at peace with those around you? If you died this week, what kind of a legacy would you leave behind?

Missionary Prayer Point: Pray that missionaries would live their lives in such a way that they might face death with no regrets.

Volunteers

> Then Jesus came to them and said, "All authority in heaven and on earth has been given to me. Therefore go and make disciples of all nations, baptizing them in the name of the Father and of the Son and of the Holy Spirit, and teaching them to obey everything I have commanded you. And surely I am with you always, to the very end of the age."
>
> Matthew 28:18–20

The woman was very obviously pregnant. In fact, she looked as if she could deliver at any time. We had set up our clinic, staffed by American volunteers, under trees around a soccer field. People would receive tickets with numbers for whichever services they needed. Then they would wait in the appropriate line. If time permitted, they could then get another ticket for another line. Today we were offering medical care, dental care, and eyeglasses.

This woman stood out in the crowd because of her size and the line of little stair-step children following her like ducklings. First she came through our medical line and obtained worm medicine for all her children. A bit later I looked up to see her having a tooth pulled with all her children gathered around her. I lost sight of her for a time in the crowd until she stopped back at my table to say good-bye. She had been to see the optometrist and was sporting a lovely pair of glasses with rhinestones in the frames. She told me good-bye and said that she was now going to the hospital to have her baby.

The hospital was about fifteen minutes away from where we were working. Within thirty minutes someone came up to me and said that the woman had already had a baby girl. She was so close to delivering that she almost gave birth on the hospital steps. Like most people in Togo, she didn't have access to routine dental, medical, and eye care. She was desperate enough to have those needs met that she almost gave birth on the ball field. Can you imagine being in labor in the extreme heat and patiently walking from line to line to receive medicine for your children, get a tooth pulled, and obtain glasses? This woman was just one example of the thousands of people who have felt the love of Christ through the many volunteers who have come overseas to serve.

Now travel with me into the mountains behind that village to another hamlet called Soumdina Haut. The scenery is spectacular when you make it to the summit. You can see a lake sparkling like a jewel in the valley. The slopes of the mountains are carefully terraced with fields of corn, tomatoes, and yams growing on them. Occasionally a majestic baobab tree raises its bare arms to the sky. It is stunningly beautiful.

While the medical team treated the sick at the clinic, the evangelism team sought to share the gospel through puppets, mime, drama, and good old-fashioned street evangelism in Soumdina Haut. The drama team was presenting a skit in which a woman was stuck in the sin box. Money could not get her out and good deeds could not get her out, and so forth the skit progressed.

Then suddenly a witch doctor stepped out of the crowd. This was not a planned part of the skit. He was covered with charms, bones, feathers, and various amulets. He carried the staff used in casting spells. He informed the audience that he was certainly powerful enough to get this poor woman out of her sin. He began to dance and chant. Brenda, the volunteer in the box, was sweltering in the heat and startled by this new development, but there was no way she was going to let this charlatan get her out of the box. He chanted and danced and pulled, but Brenda did not get out of the box. The witch doctor finally gave up.

In the finale, a man dressed as Christ came and freed her from her sin. No chants, no dances, and no spells were involved. The comparison between the power of Christ and the weakness of the witch doctor was indescribable.

We have worked with many volunteer teams during our time in Africa. Repeatedly we have seen villages that were previously closed to the gospel open up when teams come and share God's love through social ministries. Sometimes we ourselves are tired and discouraged, and working with a team of fresh volunteers rejuvenates us. We have seen volunteers themselves changed through the experience. Rarely does someone come only one time. We have seen some volunteers called to full-time Christian service. Others hesitantly came on their first trip overseas but now eagerly come once a year or more. Volunteer missions is a wonderful way to fulfill the Great Commission.

What about you? Have you considered a volunteer mission trip? It is a wonderful opportunity to give of yourself during your vacation. As you see people come to know Christ and have their needs met, you'll return to your everyday job refreshed and knowing you have made an impact on the world. If you can't go yourself, consider helping a teenager finance a trip overseas. The first time I went to Africa as a nineteen-year-old, I didn't know how I would pay for my plane ticket, but God used many older members of our church to meet my needs abundantly. God can use you also in many different ways.

Missionary Prayer Point: Pray that missionaries would be creative in their use of volunteer teams. Pray that they would seek to minister to the volunteers as well as to their targeted people group. Pray that God would use volunteer teams to raise up more missionaries to go out into the harvest.

Part 4

Natitingou Adventures—Our Move to Benin and Subsequent Stateside Assignment

(2001–2002)

Change

> See, I am doing a new thing! Now it springs up; do you not perceive it? I am making a way in the desert and streams in the wasteland.
>
> Isaiah 43:19

Change—oh, how I hate it! Some people, my husband included, seem to thrive on change. Others of us really like security and routine. It is pretty odd for me, a missionary in Africa, to hate moving so much, but it is the sad truth. So when my husband told me that he felt our time among the Kabiye was coming to an end, I did the only mature thing possible: I cried and cried and cried some more. We had worked with the Kabiye for six years. We had a comfortable routine and a nice home, and now we were considering moving to another country and another people group. Starting all over with a new language, setting up a new home (believe me, it is much more complicated to move here), and leaving all my friends seemed overwhelming to me.

John asked me to pray about it, so I did. Admittedly, in the beginning I prayed only that God would change my husband's mind, and I gave God all the reasons why we shouldn't move. Gradually, I began to listen more and talk less. My husband's dream was to start with a people group almost untouched by the gospel and be responsible for building a team to reach them with God's Word. Who was I to say no to that?

So I began to pack and hold yard sales. On January 2, 2001, we moved to Benin to begin our work among the Ditamari.

The moving company came with a large open truck to move our belongings. We looked at that truck and looked at our stuff and said there was no way everything would fit. We told the movers they would have to make two trips. They replied, "No problem. We'll make it fit." So they began to put stuff in and tie it on, put more in and tie it again, and on and on it went.

Finally, when the movers had stacked everything higher than we had ever dreamed possible, they tied the parrot cage on the pinnacle, and we were ready to begin our drive. We truly looked like the Beverly Hillbillies as we moved to Benin. Little did we know that the next few months would prove to be some of the most challenging we would ever face.

What about you? Do you resist change? The Lord says, "See, I am doing a new thing!" (Isa. 43:19). Be open to any changes, any "new thing" God may be doing in your life. Listen to your spouse and be willing to make sacrifices for his or her dream.

Missionary Prayer Point: Frequent moves and change are simply part of life on the mission field. Pray for missionaries to adjust graciously to the changes they are encountering. Pray that they would have an overwhelming sense of peace in the midst of the turbulence around them.

Trouble Begins

> O God, you are my God, earnestly I seek you; my soul thirsts for you, my body longs for you, in a dry and weary land where there is no water.
>
> Psalm 63:1

It took about eight hours to drive from Kara to our new home in Natitingou, Benin. We led the way over the bumpy, dusty road in our car full of children and pets, with the huge, swaying truck filled with all our worldly possessions following behind us. When we arrived at our new home, we were all filthy and exhausted, but the movers wanted to unload all the furniture and leave before midnight. They hauled all that dusty furniture inside and took off as quickly as they could.

While the movers carried the furniture inside, I had checked everything out and realized there was no water. "Don't worry," John said reassuringly. "It will be back on soon." We went to bed with water buckets in every shower and all the knobs turned on. All night I kept getting up and found the same problem—no running water. When we woke up the next morning, John offered to drive into town and purchase drinking water. A few minutes later he was back inside empty-handed with the words, "The car won't start."

I was really getting worried. The kids would be up soon, and we didn't have any water to give them. John decided to walk a couple of miles into town and buy some bottled water. He came back an hour later riding on the back of a motorcycle taxi carrying a case of bottled water. What a relief! However, we knew that wouldn't last long, and we were still stuck in our new home with no running water, a nonfunctioning telephone, and no transportation.

We found out very shortly that most people really did not want us there. In northern Benin, both traditional religion and Islam were strong. Although the president of Benin wanted the area evangelized, most local leaders feared losing power or money if Christianity ever really took off in the area. They subtly persecuted the missionaries or encouraged their followers to make sure missionaries did not feel welcome.

When we first arrived and let the dogs out of the car, one ran off. We knew she was off exploring and kept waiting for her to come back. Then some of our neighbors said, "Was that fat dog yours? She was really tasty." They had eaten our pet! Some people raised dogs as meat, but they were never supposed to eat someone else's pet.

When we went to the water company, they laughed and said that we could have running water in April. What exactly was I supposed to do for four months without water? We eventually were able to get the car fixed and then pay the fire brigade to fill our cistern with a load of water. You should have seen our children dance when the fire truck pulled up and began squirting water with those enormous hoses! We were thrilled to see all that water.

People's attitudes toward us were slow to change. We often felt overwhelmed by the challenges we faced while living there. We were emotionally and physically exhausted, but God was still with us. At times, it was hard to sense his presence, but he had promised to never leave us or forsake us. During these hard and lonely days, we thirsted and sought after him as we never had before. He kept his promises and was right there with us through it all.

What about you? What is your reaction to difficult times? God has promised to never abandon you, and you can trust him to keep his word regardless of your feelings. Often in the middle of those barren times in Natitingou, I felt like God was a million miles away and unaware of my pain. Over and over I had to go back to his Word and say, "God, I don't sense your presence, but you promised to be here with me. Help me, comfort me, restore me." He carried me through and will do the same for you if you will rely on him.

Missionary Prayer Point: Pray that the Holy Spirit would encourage missionaries in harsh and lonely living situations. Pray that the Lord would provide missionaries with the clean water they need to stay healthy.

Water

> Jesus answered, "Everyone who drinks this water will be thirsty again, but whoever drinks the water I give him will never thirst. Indeed, the water I give him will become in him a spring of water welling up to eternal life."
>
> John 4:13–14

You never realize how much water a family of five uses until it is in limited supply. Our cistern leaked badly, plus we used a lot of water for drinking, cooking, washing dishes, mopping, washing clothes, and even flushing the toilets, so our truckful of water was gone before we knew it. The next time we tried to buy water the fire truck was broken down, so we were forced to look for another solution. We were looking for something large enough to haul water in but small enough that we could lift it out of our vehicle. We found the perfect solution—the plastic action packers that we used as luggage when we traveled. Daily John would drive into town. At the city pump he would get in line with the ladies carrying water basins on their heads and purchase enough water for the day. After he brought it home, we would filter some of the water for drinking and ration out the rest.

The kids were allowed one small bucketful for their baths. We had a handy electric water heater that was submerged in a bucket of water. You clipped it to the side of the bucket with just the heating coil submerged. Then when the water was hot you unplugged it and removed it before getting in. The kids would bathe standing in a big basin to catch all the precious water so it would not go down the drain. After their bath, that water could be used for mopping and then finally to flush the toilet. I didn't realize how stingy we had become with our water until one night Rebekah was clean and still had about a fourth of a bucket of clean water left. I was about to confiscate the bucket and use it for bathing the next child when she snatched it back. "It's my water and I'm going to use it!" she declared as she dumped it on her head to have a good, warm, final rinse.

In the midst of this drought, it was hard to keep our focus. Why were we living with all these difficulties? We were here so that the Ditamari might come to know Christ, the living water. He had come that they might be saved, and we needed to clearly communicate that message. The story of the Samaritan woman at the well became ever more real to us as we waited in line for water in a dry, dusty place. We realized the deep desire and awe the idea of living water must have communicated to her as we tried to share that same living water with those around us.

What about you? Are you grateful for the precious gift we have in Christ? In the United States we do not usually face extreme water shortages, but sometimes our lives seem dry and empty. Pray for the living water to fill those dry places in your life and make it fruitful and vibrant.

Missionary Prayer Point: Pray that missionaries would not forget why they have come to a foreign land. Pray that they would keep the message of the gospel central to all that they do.

A Well

> Above all else, guard your heart, for it is the wellspring of life.
>
> Proverbs 4:23

Our continual discussions with the water company were producing no visible results. They told us that we might have city water in April if the rains started. This was obviously not an adequate solution. We could not live without water from December to April of every year. We had to find a long-term solution for our water issues. There was a dry well on the property that was already one hundred fifty feet deep. We consulted some "well experts," and they said they could deepen it another sixty feet. At that point we would be below the water table and should have enough water. We agreed on a price, and they showed up to begin work.

Our experts had very "modern" equipment, which consisted of metal buckets, picks, and shovels. On the hand-turned winch that was normally used to draw water, they would lower one man designated to dig with his pick and shovel. I could not fathom trusting my life to three men, a rope, and that ramshackle structure. Nevertheless, day after day they would lower him one hundred fifty feet down, and then he would send dirt up by the bucketful. It was slow, tedious work.

Every day I would go down to check on their progress. One day we began to see damp dirt being taken out of the well, and the next day it was really muddy dirt. One Thursday night they came and told us that their work was done. There was water in the well, and they could dig no farther. We paid them and gleefully ran down to our well to draw water.

I had always heard how clean well water was. We lowered our water bucket and pulled up . . . muddy water. It was not just slightly muddy water but filthy, dark brown muddy water. John hauled buckets of it to the house so I could bathe the kids, but the water was dirtier than they were! We had high hopes that the mud would settle out by the next morning. Early in the morning I traipsed down to the well only to have my hopes dashed—it was as muddy as ever.

We were supposed to drive back to Kara for the weekend, so we loaded up the vehicle and in Kara sought the advice of other missionaries who had dealt with wells. My friend Gaye told me about alum and promised that it would pull the dirt right out of the water. I asked her where I could find it and she sent me to the rock ladies in the market. (You probably thought we could just buy fruits and vegetables at our market, but there are tables piled high with all sorts of treasures.) Some ladies sold an assortment of what looked like rocks but were actually minerals with many uses. Gaye told me to ask for "the rock that cleans water."

Off to the market I went with high hopes. Unfortunately, the rock lady did not know what I was talking about. I was in a quandary—here were all these rocks, but I had no idea what alum looked like in that form. I did know what alum tasted like from my pickle-making days, and I was desperate for clean water. I did the only logical thing: I picked up a rock and stuck it to my tongue to taste it. You can imagine what is going through the rock lady's mind: "I had always heard Americans were crazy, but licking the rocks . . ." Fortunately, the first rock I tasted was the right one. When I told the lady that was the rock I wanted, she said, "Oh, you wanted alum." The word in French was identical to the English word, so I had been tasting rocks in vain!

The alum worked like magic. We would drop it into the muddy water, and within a few hours the water was crystal clear.

Similarly, even when our lives are filthy with sin we can call on Christ. His blood will purify us and make us sparkling clean.

What about you? What are you putting in the well of your life? Be careful not to pollute your life with garbage. Fill your mind with things that are pure, lovely, and wholesome.

Missionary Prayer Point: Pray for missionaries to keep their lives clean and pure. Pray that they would be careful to dwell on things that are pure and holy.

Inhospitable Landscape

> Some wandered in desert wastelands, finding no way to a city where they could settle. They were hungry and thirsty, and their lives ebbed away. Then they cried out to the Lord in their trouble, and he delivered them from their distress.
>
> Psalm 107:4–6

The last rain had fallen over six months earlier and the weather was unbelievably hot and dry. When the wind did blow, it kicked up swirling dust devils. Nothing seemed to be green and growing except the mango trees that never lost their color.

This weather was perfect for all sorts of poisonous and dangerous creatures. First we had a sudden explosion of "sun spiders" in our house. I don't know if that is their real name, but they were awful. When the heat reached its most intense peak, dozens of them suddenly appeared in the house. The spiders were large, black, hairy like a tarantula, and incredibly fast. We would be watching TV and one would scurry across the room almost before we could jump up. They ran much faster than I could, so I rarely managed to step on them. We had been told that they were poisonous enough to make you sick but not enough to kill you. To a mother of small children, those were not terribly encouraging words. We skirmished with the spiders for a couple of months, and then one day they disappeared as quickly as they had come.

The landscape was also perfect for snakes and scorpions. I'll leave the snakes for another chapter, but scorpions . . . One morning our four-year-old son Christopher went to his room, sat on the floor, and dumped out his bucket of blocks. During the night a scorpion had crawled in there unbeknownst to us. As soon as Christopher dumped the blocks, the scorpion stung him on the knee. He was in agony. He screamed and screamed as we dug out our doctor book and tried to comfort him. I read the discouraging information that this type of scorpion was painful but relatively harmless to adults. However, it could be life threatening to children aged four and under. We knew there was a Catholic hospital less than an hour away, so we piled into our vehicle and took off.

When we arrived at the hospital everyone was kind and helpful. They gave Christopher IV steroids and other medication and told us that he should be fine. He kept on screaming and was inconsolable, so they kept him there under observation. Finally they gave him a large dose of valium and said it would help him sleep, but the screaming continued unabated. They decided there wasn't anything else they could do to help him and sent us home.

I held Christopher, sang to him, and walked around carrying him until finally, eighteen hours after our ordeal had begun, he stopped crying and dozed off. The next day he got up as if nothing had happened and went right back to playing with his blocks while I was still feeling wrung out by the whole experience.

We didn't have a choice about the creatures that snuck into our house to cohabit with us, but we do have a choice in what kind of an atmosphere we encourage in our home.

What about you? Your home probably doesn't have such a physically poisonous atmosphere, but what is the emotional atmosphere? Do you seek to treat the other members of your household with kindness, making sure that encouragement flourishes there, or do you allow the insidious dangers of unkind words, gossip, and criticism poison the atmosphere of your home? Be careful what you allow into your home. Seek to make it a warm, safe place where people come to find rest.

Missionary Prayer Point: Missionaries often live in physically inhospitable places. Pray for them to be kept safe and to have wisdom in knowing how to deal with all the creatures that may seek to harm them.

Swimming

> Let us not give up meeting together, as some are in the habit of doing, but let us encourage one another—and all the more as you see the Day approaching.
>
> Hebrews 10:25

I sat shivering by the pool, drinking hot chocolate. Being cold was such a delicious feeling. The sun on the pool was sparkling. It was a chilly January day with a temperature of about seventy-eight degrees. (After months of temperatures over one hundred degrees, I feel cold when it gets below eighty.) You may be wondering what in the world I was doing at the pool when I was so cold that I needed hot chocolate to warm up my insides.

God created us with a need for fellowship. In Africa, just like in America, I readily recognized the need for friends. That was why I was at the pool. Every Friday afternoon a small group of women gathered there with their kids. We were all from different denominations, we had different jobs, and some of us were even from different countries, but we were all missionary women serving for the same purpose—to see people come to know Christ. We all dealt daily with the same frustrations—language barriers, lack of privacy, challenges with children's schooling, and cooking with limited ingredients. Some of us were rather reserved and quiet, others were fairly loud and silly. Some loved cooking and entertaining, and others did everything possible to get out of it. Some were married and some were single. We were all extremely different.

As I shivered and drank hot chocolate, I enjoyed fellowship and lots of dialogue with my friends. Conversations ranged from very serious, teary discussions over problems with children or sick family back home to silly jokes. One missionary in our midst had an incredible sense of time. Every so often we would ask, "What time is it, Edith?" She was usually right on the dot—without a watch. We laughed and told stories of crazy happenings during the week. Every so often we took a break and played games with the kids such as Marco Polo or Sharks and Minnows. After all, our husbands thought we were there to get some exercise.

Every so often we began to feel claustrophobic and looked around to see that our dozen or so children had snuck up to try to overhear what we were saying. We would tell them, "Kids, back to your own table!" The kids even brought card games and books to the pool because they learned that this was Mama's time.

We did not have a ladies' ministry or Sunday school class or support group geared to meet our needs, but we chose to set aside this weekly time to simply celebrate our friendship. When I moved to Benin, I still came back to Togo about once a month to be with my friends. Our group shifted and changed as people came and went from the mission field, but I think this weekly get-together was part of the secret of our longevity.

Our fellowship didn't stop at the pool. During the week we all knew we could call on each other. When I was pregnant and incredibly sick, one of these women would often come to my rescue. If John was staying late in the village, she would carry my kids home with her and feed them supper. I often gave vaccinations to my friends' children or cooked holiday meals for them. We all looked out for each other.

Friendship is an incredible gift. To cultivate it we have to invest time and energy. We have to be willing to be vulnerable and transparent. A true friend can make our life's journey happier and healthier.

What about you? Do you have any close friends outside of your family? We live in such a busy, hectic world that we have to consciously, deliberately pursue friendships. They are well worth the investment of time and energy.

Missionary Prayer Point: Pray that God would provide missionaries with at least one close friend to help them carry their load.

Midnight Drive

> Some trust in chariots and some in horses, but we trust in the name of the Lord our God.
>
> Psalm 20:7

In Benin people are not supposed to drive after dark, especially in the northern part of the country where we lived. Robbers in northern Benin had copied the methods of the highway bandits of the nineteenth century. On a narrow stretch of road they would place a roadblock and rob any hapless travelers who chose to travel at night and were forced to stop at the roadblock. Of course, the military also frowned on people traveling at night and set up roadblocks as well to try to limit travel. In Benin people simply do not make long drives after dark.

One day Christopher got between his puppy and the puppy's supper, and the dog bit him. We cleaned the bite and didn't think much of it except a passing concern because the dog had been too young to be vaccinated for rabies. We knew there had been an outbreak of rabies in the area, but the vet wasn't concerned, so we didn't see any reason for concern. Then about a week after the bite the dog started acting strange. He began to growl and snarl. All night long he howled and carried on. He finally began having seizures the following day and then died. The vet told us that the dog had apparently died of rabies and we should seek treatment for Christopher immediately. He needed the first shot within ten to twelve days of being bitten and nine days had already passed.

It was late afternoon, but John and I felt that our only option was to begin driving to the capital immediately. We left the house at dusk, carrying hastily packed luggage, three cranky children, and the dead dog in case they needed to autopsy him. Every few miles we encountered soldiers. We would repeatedly say, "My child needs to get to the doctor." They would shine their lights through the car, see the children, and wave us on. Over and over this scenario would repeat itself. We would see a roadblock and approach it slowly with fear in our hearts. Repeatedly the soldiers were kind and sent us on our way.

The night was dark in a way most Americans have a hard time imagining. There were no streetlights or any other lights in the pitch black. As we went by people's homes, we would occasionally see a cooking fire or a kerosene lantern. The road was rough and potholed, and the going was very slow. By midnight we had traveled only as far as we would normally travel in two hours of daylight. We realized we had to stop at a hotel for the night and continue on in the morning.

God watched over us and protected us through that harrowing drive. He enabled us to make it to the capital in record time the next morning. Even through the darkest night, we can know that we are not alone. God is with us, and he will watch over us. Isn't it comforting to know that we don't face any trial alone?

What about you? Are you aware of the presence of God in your day-to-day life? When you are afraid, discouraged, or in pain, choose to seek God's presence. "Never will I leave you" is his promise to us. We can trust him and cling to him even in difficult times.

Missionary Prayer Point: Pray for missionaries to really practice living consciously in God's presence. Pray that they would be very aware of his comforting presence in their day-to-day lives. Pray for their safety from thieves and other dangers that they face.

Flight to Paris

> Be strong and courageous. Do not be afraid or terrified because of them, for the LORD your God goes with you; he will never leave you nor forsake you.
>
> Deuteronomy 31:6

The next morning we arrived in the capital city of Cotonou by 11:30 a.m. We breathed a sigh of relief knowing that once more disaster had been averted. Our business facilitator had already purchased the serum we needed. All we had to do was get to the doctor's office before she closed for lunch and our troubles would be over.

I nervously paced the doctor's crowded waiting room. I knew everyone else had gotten there first, but we had driven almost all night to get there. Surely this rabid-dog bite constituted some sort of an emergency and ought to get us bumped up to the front of the line. Apparently no one agreed with us, so we sat there with our anti-rabies serum on ice for over an hour before Dr. Tijani could see us. I must admit that I waited impatiently. With all that adrenaline from the last twenty-four hours, I just couldn't relax. I kept feeling like something else would go wrong. It could not possibly be this simple to treat such a potentially life-threatening problem.

We finally made it into Dr. Tijani's inner sanctum. She carefully inspected the medicine, paused, and then began to speak. Her words caused my heart to sink. "I was afraid of this. This is a horse-based serum and carries a high risk of life-threatening shock. We have no life support available here. If it were my child, I would never consider giving him this medicine."

"What would you do?" John and I asked. She replied, "I would do everything possible to get my child to Europe where there is suitable medicine." There was no point in any further discussion. We knew that there were only three flights a week and one of them was leaving Benin that very evening. We called our business manager, and everyone began working at high speed.

Our mission board had no qualms about sending us to Europe for treatment. Their physician's only qualifier was that Christopher had to get the medicine within twenty-four hours. If we couldn't get out of the country in that period, we had to use the horse-based serum and take our chances. It was essential that Christopher get treatment immediately because the time frame for treating rabies was running out.

The airlines required us to get validation of a true emergency from the airline physician before they would bump passengers to make room for the patient and a parent. John, Christopher, and Judy (our business manager) immediately went to the physician's office and obtained clearance. She agreed that it was an emergency but wanted to get the dog's head tested to be certain that it really was rabies. Unfortunately, the closest testing facility was in France, almost two thousand miles away. The airline doctor, mission board doctor, and insurance company discussed carrying the dog's head in the carry-on luggage, but the idea of the customs officers finding it caused the airline physician to change her mind. Her droll comment was, "I can just see the customs officers asking, 'What kind of traffic is this?' and detaining you. That would not be helpful." We were finally able to bury the dead dog who had been traveling all this way with us.

Armed with the official doctor's certificate, John and Judy went to the Air France office. They were allowed to purchase two tickets for the flight leaving that evening. While they were waiting on the tickets to be printed, two very angry tourists came in. They had been bumped from the flight and were going to be stuck in Cotonou for a few more days. John and Judy very wisely kept their silence in the corner as they realized this was how John and Christopher were able to get seats.

Just a couple of hours later, in a mad flurry we sent John and Christopher to the airport with just a carry-on bag, medical records, and the address of a good hospital in Paris. It was hard to let them go, but I felt relief knowing that finally Christopher was being taken care of. They spent about a week in Paris, and Christopher received the medical care he needed.

What about you? You probably are not dealing with a rabid dog, but do you trust God to help you find a solution to whatever problem you are facing? He is faithful and will provide for you.

Missionary Prayer Point: Pray for missionaries to be kept safe from dangerous critters such as snakes and rabid animals. Pray that in case of an emergency, God will provide a way to get access to good medical care.

Mystery Meat

> So do not worry, saying, "What shall we eat?" or "What shall we drink?" or "What shall we wear?" For the pagans run after all these things, and your heavenly Father knows that you need them. But seek first his kingdom and his righteousness, and all these things will be given to you as well.
>
> Matthew 6:31–33

I like meat. All my life, our main meal usually involved meat of some kind in some form. It might just be a little hamburger in a casserole, but there was meat. When we moved to Natitingou, it became obvious that something was going to have to change.

Within a couple of days of our arrival, I drove around until I found the meat market. It was easy to find; I just followed the vultures. The building had vultures circling overhead, quite a few perched on the roof, and some even hopping in the dirt looking for some tidbit left from the morning. The building looked like a jail in an old Western movie. It was a short, dark building with heavy metal doors and bars on the windows. There was no electricity and no refrigeration. The heavy doors and bars should have given me a clue that this town considered meat a pretty valuable commodity.

I showed up the next morning ready to purchase my meat. Unfortunately, by the time I got there a long line had formed. I waited and waited. I finally got up to the counter and was told that they were out of meat. I could see meat right there on the counter, but they insisted it had already been sold. They told me to try again tomorrow. I decided that the next day I would get there really early.

The next morning I got up at daybreak and went to the meat market. I beat everyone there, even the butchers. I sat on the roots of a huge tree and watched the sunrise with my friends the buzzards. After a while a very old, rusty rattletrap of a pickup truck barreled up to the meat market. About half a dozen men hopped out and lifted out a beautiful sight—the carcass of a dead cow. They set to work with knives and machetes as a crowd of women gathered around. Bits of bone and gristle flew in the air to be snatched by the hovering vultures.

When the men had the meat carved into chunks, they carried it into the building to sell. I hurried inside only to be told, "Just a moment." Everyone else was able to buy their meat, but none was available for me. After a few days it became obvious that they simply were not going to sell me any meat, so I became creative. I sent the Ditamari lady who helped me around the house to buy the meat for me. Guess what? The market men said, "You work for that white lady, don't you? No meat." I even sent the yard worker, thinking they wouldn't recognize him, but no luck.

We finally resorted to driving all the way to Kara every other weekend to buy groceries. The meat was freshly killed and we couldn't freeze it for the trip home, so we could only bring it home in small quantities. We adapted. I learned to cook a whole slew of vegetarian recipes. I learned to cook regular recipes with very little meat in them. It was probably much healthier for us. We certainly all lost some weight.

Some time later we wanted to have a special party for the orphans in town. I asked them, "What would you like us to fix—spaghetti, rice, or couscous?" Imagine my chagrin when they answered, "Meat. We don't care what you fix with it, but we want meat." I warned them not to get their hopes up but that I would try to get some meat.

The next morning, with very low expectations I walked up to the meat counter. "I need twenty-five pounds of meat, please."

Now, keep in mind that previously they wouldn't sell me one or two pounds. I expected to be laughed out of the market. I watched in amazement as they cut up and weighed twenty-five pounds of boneless beef without any discussion. That night we had a huge celebration, and every single child had plenty of meat. I realized that God really does care about the "least of these," even giving them the meat they had longed for.

When we returned to the United States that fall, the children's grandmother was amused when at the end of every meal the kids would say, "Nanny, thank you for all that good meat." She tried to explain that it would be more correct to say "pork chops" or "roast" or so forth, but to my excited children, it was meat and lots of it!

What about you? Do you realize that all you have comes from God? You really don't have to worry about what you will eat or what you will wear. God knows that you need these things, and he delights in providing them for his children. If he could give the orphans meat in that meatless town, surely he can meet your needs.

Missionary Prayer Point: Pray that missionaries would not live in fear but that they would confidently rely on God to meet all their needs. He really does care about material needs as well as spiritual ones.

Snake Story

> The LORD watches over you—the LORD is your shade at your right hand; the sun will not harm you by day, nor the moon by night. The LORD will keep you from all harm—he will watch over your life; the LORD will watch over your coming and going both now and forevermore.
>
> Psalm 121:5–8

You can't be a good missionary without a good snake story, right? When we speak at churches, invariably someone will ask, "Can you tell us a snake story from Africa?" It would be terribly embarrassing if I had to admit that I did not have such a story, so let me share a few of my snake stories with you.

The first snake that I remember seeing in Togo was draped across my husband's desk. I was walking toward his desk, not really paying attention to it. I tossed some Bible correspondence courses on his desk, and it looked like the entire desk moved. It took me a second to realize that a huge snake had been sunning itself on the desk. John was gone, but Ray, an older missionary who had dropped off the courses, came to my rescue. That snake may have been long and skinny, but it was fast. It darted from side to side in the room and Ray gave chase. Finally, with a mighty thump of his cane, he dispatched that snake. Once it was dead, we realized that the snake was over six feet long but only about one inch in diameter. It must have snuck under the door.

Another night John was driving along a rarely used dirt road when he saw what he thought was a log laying across the road.

Then the "log" slowly turned and rose up to look at him, and he realized that it was a huge python. The pastor with him shouted, "Run over it!" John did so, but the snake was so big it was almost like running over a telephone pole. Even after being run over, the snake was moving toward the bush. The pastor was really excited and exclaimed, "We have to get out and chase him. That is a lot of really good meat getting away!" John informed him that there was no way he was getting out of the car in the dark to chase a very angry snake that was bigger than he was. He drove on without letting anyone out to chase the snake.

My last story is my favorite. It just shows how mighty God is and how he protects his children. It was a day set aside to pray for West Africa. We knew that on that day thousands of people were praying for us. The girls did their schoolwork while four-year-old Christopher jumped on the trampoline right outside our door. It was a short children's trampoline, but Christopher was a little boy, so he had dragged a chair beside it to climb on. All day long he had done the same routine—climb on the chair to the trampoline, jump a few times, jump off, run around the trampoline, climb back on the chair. Around and around he went, using his boundless supply of energy.

Finally his sisters finished their schoolwork and went out to join him. I was cooking dinner and watching them through the window when I saw Sarah pick up a huge rock and throw it toward her brother. I dashed out the door, shouting, "Sarah Joy Crocker, you stop that right now!" She picked up another rock and threw it.

By this time I made it to the trampoline and found that she had killed a viper. A viper is a very small, very poisonous snake. It partially buries itself in the dirt, making itself almost invisible until it suddenly darts after its prey. It had apparently been sleeping under Christopher's chair. My barefoot boy had been climbing over it all day long. When it started chasing him, Sarah was right there. She immediately began throwing stones at it. She very effectively protected her brother by killing it. We made a big deal out of it and dubbed her "Sarah the Valiant

Snake Killer!" If that snake had bitten any of my children, they would have died before we could reach medical care. Truly God is our protector, and he watches over us day and night.

What about you? Do you live a life of fear, or do you consciously realize that God is your protector? Choose to praise him for his care for you, and live confidently knowing that he constantly watches over you.

Missionary Prayer Point: Pray for God's protection over missionaries from snakes, diseases, thieves, and whatever else may be threatening them. Pray that they would live at ease without fear of harm because of God's care over them.

AIDS

> The cords of death entangled me; the torrents of destruction overwhelmed me. The cords of the grave coiled around me; the snares of death confronted me. In my distress I called to the Lord; I cried to my God for help. From his temple he heard my voice; my cry came before him, into his ears.
>
> Psalm 18:4–6

I looked at the rusty, well-used razor on the bathroom sink and felt my world collapse around me. I had just undergone an emergency appendectomy at Clinique Mahuna in Benin. Now as I looked at that razor that had cut me as the doctors prepped me for surgery the previous day, I realized that it was used on every surgery patient. It had not even been wiped with alcohol, just rinsed in the sink. What about the IV catheters or all the needles I had been poked with in the last twenty-four hours? Had they been new or used?

A few years earlier I had worked at a local hospital for six weeks to earn my license to practice nursing in Africa. One day I watched my supervisor give twenty-three people injections with the same needle and syringe. He occasionally rinsed it out, but it was too much trouble to even change the needle. I knew I lived in a country where the published HIV infection rate was 13 percent, and in reality it was probably much higher. For years I had assiduously avoided the hospital, and now I had allowed the doctors to perform surgery on me.

It had all begun two days earlier. We had driven to the capital city all packed and ready for a trip to Singapore for training to become strategy coordinators for our mission. I had been feeling slightly uncomfortable and nauseated all day. Gradually my pain worsened until I was in agony. I woke my husband and asked him to get help. We found someone to stay with the children and began our search for help.

The streets were eerily deserted at three a.m. At one point a gang of rough-looking men had barricaded the road, and John drove quickly onto the sidewalk to avoid being detained by them. When we arrived at the doctor's, she was sound asleep in bed. "Help! My wife's dying!" shouted my husband. "Go away! My wife's asleep!" replied the doctor's husband. John kept calling for help until the doctor agreed to see us. She gave me a couple of pain shots but finally told John that I probably needed surgery. She directed us to the Clinique Mahuna, which had a surgical suite and was a better option than the public hospital.

Since some of the machines were out of order at the clinic, it was a long day as we went from place to place to get diagnostic work done. Everywhere we went I had to gingerly hobble out to our pickup truck, holding my IV bottle, and then ride on bumpy, potholed, dirt roads to the next laboratory.

In a God-ordained "coincidence," an American doctor named Dr. Bailey was in town working with a volunteer mission team. He came to the hospital to see me and went with me every step of the way. He was a surgeon, but the hospital would not agree for him to use their operating room. I would not agree to have surgery if he wasn't present, so the hospital and I reached a compromise: Dr. Bailey would assist the hospital's surgeon.

The staff wasted little time in prepping me for surgery and carrying me to the operating room. I laid there tied to the table and talked to Dr. Bailey as we waited for the hospital staff. We amused ourselves by counting the mosquitoes buzzing around the bright lights.

The doctors finally came and put me to sleep. Dr. Bailey told me later that the surgeon made the incision and began pulling out my intestines hunting for my appendix. Dr. Bailey didn't speak any French, so in his best Louisiana accent he said, "Well, look at that! It's her appendix." He reached over and simply performed the rest of the surgery himself.

I knew God had provided for me in miraculously sending Dr. Bailey to help me. When after the surgery I had some problems with infection and malaria, he agreed to stay while the rest of his team went home. I was thankful to have survived surgery in an African hospital, but I was terrified that now I would die a lingering death from AIDS. I was in physical pain from the surgery, and emotionally I felt like I could not handle any more. We had already survived meningitis, scorpions, and a bite by a rabid dog, and we often lived without water in a hostile place. Wasn't that enough? We left for our stateside assignment (furlough) a few weeks later, but I was still hurting and questioning.

Over and over during our time in the USA, I turned to the psalms and read about God being my refuge. It was only by meditating on his Word that I was able to find a semblance of peace during the six months of HIV testing that I underwent. You cannot imagine my relief when the last test came back negative and I was cleared. God had been my refuge, and although I felt battle scarred and incredibly weary, I had survived by hiding in him.

What about you? When troubles come into your life, how do you respond? It is okay to question God and to be brutally honest with him about your feelings. Read the book of Psalms. You will be amazed at how honest David was about his feelings, yet he continued to praise God for who he was in the midst of pain. We should follow his example.

Missionary Prayer Point: Missionaries are vulnerable to depression and intense emotional pain. Pray for them to find refuge in God regardless of the difficulty they are facing.

Autism

> I praise you because I am fearfully and wonderfully made; your works are wonderful, I know that full well. My frame was not hidden from you when I was made in the secret place. When I was woven together in the depths of the earth, your eyes saw my unformed body. All the days ordained for me were written in your book before one of them came to be.
>
> Psalm 139:14–16

I drove home from Emory University Hospital in Atlanta with Christopher safely buckled into the backseat. I couldn't stop crying. *Autism? There has to be some mistake. My child can't be autistic.* But deep down inside I knew there was no mistake.

I thought back through the years. As a baby, Christopher had been incredibly content. He was a chubby baby who didn't demand a lot of attention. The whole family loved playing with him, but he was just as content to entertain himself. He was late sitting up and crawling, but then in a developmental burst he learned to sit up, crawl, walk, run, and climb all in a one-month period. I breathed a sigh of relief because he seemed to be catching up developmentally. At eighteen months he began to talk. He was finally completely on track. All my worrying had been for nothing.

Then gradually Christopher quit talking and seemed to withdraw. He was very active and agile, but he no longer spoke. We shared our concerns with any doctor we could find, and finally our mission board sent us to another country to have his hearing checked. The doctor informed us that he could hear better than we could and sent us on our way. Six months later we traveled back again to be told, "Look, your child can walk. What more do you want?" What I wanted was for my son to talk, interact with me, and develop like everyone else's child seemed to do.

When he turned three and still wasn't talking much, we took a short vacation to the United States in hopes of finding some answers. The pediatrician just brushed aside my worries, telling me that lots of three-year-old boys don't talk. "He's just a little hyperactive and too busy to talk much. Also, he's being exposed to many languages, and that may confuse him, slowing his language development." Being somewhat reassured, we went back to the mission field, but I noticed that all the other missionary kids were speaking English and didn't seem confused by all the languages. Why not mine?

Christopher would often become obsessed with one particular thing at a time, so I would try to use that to teach him. At one point our dog had puppies, and he was totally wrapped up in one of the puppies. Everywhere Christopher went he carried that little puppy. I was concerned that he would never listen to stories, so one day I told him, "You know, books help children get smarter. I bet if we read stories to your puppy, he would get smarter too." From that day on the puppy would have story time every day. Christopher would sit by me and hold his puppy where it could see the book, and I would read to the puppy. After a few months the dog weighed as much as Christopher and could no longer sit on his lap, but by that time Christopher was hooked on stories and would sit and listen to us read.

When he was four and a half years old, I finally found a doctor who would listen to me. He directed me to set up an appointment with a pediatric neuropsychiatrist. That search had brought us to Emory. John had a speaking engagement at a World Missions Conference. He had offered to cancel and come with me, but I was sure this was just a preliminary appointment. We would do some tests and go home. At a later date John and I would come back for further appointments and evaluations before a diagnosis was made.

After a two-hour appointment, the doctor told me that it was obvious my son had a mild form of autism called PDD-NOS. He said there was no treatment or cure, and at this point medication wouldn't help the symptoms. No further appointments were necessary. I was given the phone number for the Emory Autism Resource Center and sent on my way.

Now I was reeling. *Autism*. Just the word is so emotionally charged. It brings up so many images and fears. There were so many unanswered questions: Would he hold a job? Live alone as an adult? Always be dependent on us? And what about us? Would we be able to return to the mission field? Could we access the help we needed overseas? On and on the litany of questions went. I didn't have an epiphany or any sudden answer; in fact, some of my questions are still unanswered. Even staying on the mission field has become a year-by-year decision.

As I laid on my bed, walked, drove, or wept, I poured out my fears and pain to God. I didn't immediately receive peace, and there are days when I still struggle. Yet I know that God has heard me, and I'm not going through this struggle alone. God was not shocked by Christopher's diagnosis because God created him and he is precious to God. Over and over I carry my pain to God and rest in the promise that he will never leave us alone. He will walk through this valley alongside us.

What about you? How involved are you with people with disabilities? If you see them struggle, do you try to help or do you turn away, pretending not to see? Have you taken time to get to know as a friend someone with a disability? Everyone is a precious creation of God, and we need to treat them as such. Consider starting a Sunday school class for children or adults with disabilities who might not understand the lesson in a regular class. Offer to care for a child with a disability for an evening to give the parents a rest. Take a risk and get involved.

Missionary Prayer Point: Missionaries who have children with disabilities struggle to stay on the field due to a lack of medical and educational services available where they serve. Pray that they would be wise in balancing their call to missions and their children's needs. Pray that they would be creative in finding ways to meet their children's needs.

Part 5

Return to Togo

(2002–2005)

Return to Togo

> They cried to you and were saved; in you they trusted and were not disappointed.
>
> Psalm 22:5

I felt totally overwhelmed at the idea of returning to the mission field after our time in the United States. Between the isolation and all the crises we had lived through in Benin, I thought that I might lose my mind if I went back. The idea of trying to survive in that kind of loneliness for four more years . . . I could hardly fathom it. I knew God had called us to the mission field, but for the first time I dreaded going back. Then our mission board stepped in. "We don't want you to feel pressured, but if you will write a request we'll try to help you recruit a special education teacher." Feel pressured? I was ecstatic. We wrote up the request and began sending emails, trying to find a teacher.

In January we went to a conference at the Missionary Learning Center in Virginia. A group of volunteers looking for jobs passed through. One young woman, LaVerne Brown, felt pulled toward our request. It was totally different from anything she had really considered, so she laid out a fleece before the Lord. "I'll consider this, Lord, but only if you provide some way for me to meet these children first." Having prayed that, she felt pretty safe until Larry, our stateside administrator, asked her if she would like to meet us. "What do you mean?" she replied. "They're in Africa!" When she found out we were there for the weekend, she knew she would be returning to Africa with us.

That was a huge relief to me. I would no longer be responsible for educating all of my children, and I would have at least one other American woman in Natitingou with me. In spite of this, every time I considered returning to Benin, I felt overwhelmed with dread. My prayer journal during that time says over and over, "I just don't think I can do it. Please give me courage. I don't know if I can face living there again." On and on I would honestly pour out before God my pain, anger, and dread at going back. I felt that he would either change my feelings or my situation. He had already provided a teacher; I knew he was capable of doing much more.

A few months before our scheduled departure we received a call from the medical department of our mission board. "Mrs. Crocker, I'm sorry to have to tell you this, but there is no way we can approve your family living in an isolated setting. Your son may never achieve fluency in English if you do. You will have to relocate to a town with at least twenty American children." He thought he was delivering bad news, but it was all I could do to keep from dancing a jig. I was so relieved. As it turned out, we were able to keep working with the Ditamari people. We simply moved back to Kara, Togo, where there was a large American population.

The icing on the cake was the house God provided for us. We had requested that our business facilitator try to find something close to the Wycliffe Bible Translator's conference center. The director there had five children and our families were very close. The center had a lot of recreational options, and having ready access to it would provide the socialization my children needed. I was doubtful that anything could be found close to it, but I committed the matter to prayer. Then we received word from our business facilitator. "Would you be 'close enough' if a very weak girl throwing a baseball could hit the building?" She had found a brand-new house right across the street from the center. We had never lived in a new house before. This one was perfect.

When agonizing over decisions, it is easy to forget that God really does care about the details. When I was confused about the future and reeling from all the disasters we seemed to be facing, I often felt like shouting, "Are you listening, God? Do you care at all what I'm going through?" Over and over his Word assured me that he did care and he would answer at the right time. That's what I offer to you regardless of your situation: God is listening and he will answer. He cares for you infinitely beyond what you can imagine.

What about you? Have you given up on sharing your cares, worries, and fears with God? You can be honest with him. He loves you and longs to comfort you.

Missionary Prayer Point: Pray that missionaries would be transparent with God. Pray that they would be comforted in every situation they face by the comfort found in Christ.

A New Thing

> He settles the barren woman in her home as a happy mother of children. Praise the LORD.
>
> Psalm 113:9

Sarah came and sat beside me at the table. "Mom?"

"Yes?" I replied.

"Can I ask you something?"

"Of course, honey."

"Can we adopt another baby?" (At this point, God had given us all three of our children by adoption.)

"I wish we could, but we won't be going back to the USA for three and a half years. By that point you will be a teenager, and I don't know if we'll be ready to start over with a baby."

"What if I prayed and God just gave us a baby? Would you be mad?"

"No. Children are a gift from God, but don't get your hopes up because babies are very rare." How do you let your kids down gently? You want them to have faith and ask God for big things, but some things just aren't possible—like God just giving us a baby. Soon after God allowed us to adopt Sarah, I had stopped praying to get pregnant. I was completely at peace with the way God had chosen to put our family together.

Then I became sick. It started as just a little nausea, but it got worse and worse. I finally couldn't even keep water down. In a week's time I had lost ten pounds. I finally was so weak that I couldn't get out of bed. A friend asked me, "Do you think you could be pregnant?"

"Please don't tease me about that. For almost fifteen years I have been repeatedly disappointed, thinking I might be pregnant. I went through infertility treatment and all that. I assure you that I am not pregnant, and it is not something I want to discuss." My friend dropped the subject but convinced John to get me south to the doctor.

The next morning my family loaded me into the car as I protested I would get better if everybody would just leave me alone. When I got to the hospital the doctor immediately asked if I could be pregnant. Once more I explained why it was unlikely, and he agreed. The staff admitted me to the hospital and began an IV to get some fluids in me. They drew blood and ran tests. They couldn't find anything wrong, so they ran even more tests. The doctor was puzzled. "We can't find anything wrong with you, but you can't stop throwing up. We're going to go ahead and do a pregnancy test just to be sure." A bit later he came in and told me, "We finally found out what's wrong with you. What do you want to name him?" Words can't begin to express the shock and elation that we experienced.

A couple minutes later Christopher came running into the room ahead of his sisters. "Go tell your sisters that Mama is having a baby!" He went running out, and we could hear him excitedly telling the girls. Their immediate response was, "Christopher Crocker, you are lying! Mama is sick." When they found out it really was true, they were thrilled. "God heard my prayer! He really heard my prayer!" was Sarah's response.

Being pregnant was such a surprise and such a gift. It was just one more example of God's power. I had so little faith, but my daughter believed God could answer her prayers for a sibling. For whatever reason, God in his sovereignty said yes to her prayers and gave us another son.

God knew our hearts' desire. We had longed for a large family and didn't see how it would be possible. Bit by bit God has enlarged our family.

What about you? What are you trusting God for? Are you praying and seeking his will? He is all-powerful, and it will surprise you what he can do and will do when you pray in faith. Believe God and trust him to answer your prayers, even when it seems impossible.

Missionary Prayer Point: Pray that missionaries would be faithful in prayer and that they would trust God to do great things.

Campsite "Thieves"

> So do not fear, for I am with you; do not be dismayed, for I am your God. I will strengthen you and help you; I will uphold you with my righteous right hand.
>
> Isaiah 41:10

Wilderness camping—just what every pregnant woman dreams of doing. I had been nauseated for months, but finally at five months the nausea was letting up a little, and I felt like I could function again. The kids and John were dying to go camping, so I began to pack. Keep in mind that there was absolutely nothing available at the campsite. We would have to bring not only our tent and sleeping bags but all drinking water, snacks, charcoal, grill, and anything else we might need.

The truck was very full by the time the five of us were ready to get in. We left around noon, and by the time we crossed the border to Benin and arrived at the camping area, it was late afternoon. We had to hustle to get our tent up and the lanterns lit before we were in pitch dark. Rebekah kept insisting that she saw baboons sticking their heads over the edge of the cliff to look at us, but we were sure they were a figment of her imagination. After all, none of us had seen them. We grilled our supper, made hot chocolate, and went to bed. I was very worn out, and it was cool and pleasant camping near the stream, so I slept soundly that night.

Early the next morning I made the uncomfortable discovery that Rebekah was right. There really was a baboon family observing our campsite. They came fairly close to us, so we could see they were beautiful creatures.

Not long after sunrise all the kids were up and about helping build campfires. After everyone was fed and dressed, we began our day of adventure. We hiked, swam in the waterfall, picnicked, and had a simply fabulous day. That night we sat around the campfire feeling very relaxed and happy. We went to sleep before the moon came up.

I woke up a couple hours later, needing to use the "restroom" in the woods. As I unzipped the tent, I noticed that there was a light shining in the back of the pickup truck. Robbers! Here we were stuck in the middle of nowhere with no way to defend ourselves. I did what any red-blooded American female would do: I woke up my husband. "John, there are burglars in the truck. What are we going to do?" He told me to lie very still and pretend that I was asleep. (Most robberies here are nonconfrontational. As long as no one got hurt, they could have whatever was in that truck.)

Now this pregnant lady had a very full bladder and desperately needed to get out of the tent, but whenever I would lift up my head, the light was still on in the back of the truck. We could see it shining around the edge of the cover on the vehicle. John would whisper to me to be still, I would sneak another peek, and back and forth it went.

Finally I could stand it no longer. I unzipped the tent and tiptoed into the woods. John snuck over to the truck to see what was happening. Guess what? My burglars were nonexistent! A full moon had risen and was shining through the truck. We had a good laugh, and since we were wide awake we sat and enjoyed the play of moonlight on the stream. It was a beautiful, romantic night.

Too often we react to fear by ignoring it and hoping it will go away. Often, if we'll face our fears, they will disappear in the light of day. Don't waste your energy on worry. God is in control.

What about you? Are you controlled by fears and worries? Confront your fears and watch them melt away in the light of God's love.

Missionary Prayer Point: Pray that missionaries would live lives of power and love. Pray that they would not be controlled by fear.

Midnight Crisis

> I prayed for this child, and the Lord has granted me what I asked of him. So now I give him to the Lord.
>
> 1 Samuel 1:27–28

I woke up in pain. I was six months pregnant and had read that I would start feeling more uncomfortable as I got further along, but this seemed so intense. I walked up and down the hall for a few hours and felt better. I didn't mention it to anyone. Who wants to listen to a pregnant woman complain all the time?

The next night I woke up at exactly the same time. The pain was very intense, but after a few hours it eased off. At that point I emailed a physician in the United States. After a third night I decided it was time to drive five hours to the hospital and see what the doctor said. It was time for another checkup anyway. I still wasn't worried. I grabbed an overnight bag and our family drove down to the hospital. The next morning we saw the doctor, and he gave me the startling news that I was having contractions and had already begun dilating. He told me that if I didn't get back to America or France, my baby would die. He told me that I could travel by commercial airliner but that I should leave as quickly as possible. They gave me some medicine to try to stop the contractions and sent me on my way.

We went back to the hospital's guesthouse to load up our things and drive to Lome. I was bemoaning the fact that we had packed so lightly since we had expected to go home that day. I really wanted to disguise the fact that I was pregnant so I wouldn't get put off the plane along the way. If the airline knew

I was in labor, they would never let me fly. The guesthouse hostess, a missionary who oversaw the small inn for guests at the hospital, said, "Hang on a minute. I have just the thing!" She went to her room and came back with a voluminous green dress made out of soft knit. It was perfect. Not only was it comfortable, but it definitely concealed my pregnant figure.

Meanwhile our fellow missionaries went to work. Our business facilitator managed to get us five plane tickets to the United States for the next day. There are only three international flights a week, and often there is a waiting list, so this was definitely a miracle. As we drove directly to the capital city, our teacher, LaVerne, went to our home and packed trunks with our clothes and computer. Two other friends drove seven hours to get the trunks to us. We had to go to the airport at 4:30 p.m. We knew the trunks were coming, but we weren't sure if they would make it before we had to catch our flight. They got there at 4:15, and we quickly loaded them up and drove to the airport.

Everything went smoothly until we got to Cincinnati. I was exhausted and having more contractions. I thought my water had broken and I was going to lose the baby. I finally sat down in the airport and just cried. I probably should have gone immediately to the hospital at that point, but I wanted to get home and be with family during this crisis. I was afraid if I went to the hospital, they would not let me travel and I would be stuck in Cincinnati for the remainder of the pregnancy, or if the baby were born he would be in NICU there for months.

John found a flight to Huntsville that was leaving immediately and would be there in forty-five minutes. It still had a seat left. I hurried onto the plane, leaving John and the kids at the airport. Once we were airborne, our family let the airport know that I was on the flight and in labor. It was one of those small planes with only twenty seats. You can imagine the pilot's reaction: "What do you mean I have a lady in labor on this flight?"

I made it to Huntsville, and as I got off the plane I saw a policeman with a wheelchair. I wondered who it was for but kept walking. When Dianne, a friend who picked me up since our family was all out of town, spotted me, she called the policeman over. He wheeled me to the vehicle, and we drove quickly to the hospital. My doctor was waiting there for me. I was so relieved to find that my water had not broken and that the baby wasn't coming yet.

With a lot of medication, bed rest, several hospitalizations, and much prayer, we were able to hold off the baby's birth for a while longer. I arrived in the United States only twenty-five weeks pregnant, and the baby wasn't born until I was at thirty-six weeks, only a month early. You can't imagine our joy as we met our miracle son. We named him Benjamin Paul Crocker and gratefully received him into our family. Truly he was a gift of God's grace.

What about you? What is your reaction to times of stress and crisis? Do you panic or turn to Christ for strength? He formed us and knows us intimately. We can trust him to see us through anything.

Missionary Prayer Point: Pray for any missionaries you know who are pregnant. Pray that God would protect both the mom and the baby and enable them to have the medical care they need.

Abidjan Coup

> I will lie down and sleep in peace, for you alone, O Lord, make me dwell in safety.
>
> Psalm 4:8

I lay on the floor of the room surrounded by my children. Over the staccato bursts of automatic gunfire I heard the roar of the mob. I knew we were going to die.

Two weeks earlier our family had flown to Abidjan to begin our training to become strategy coordinators. We had been trying to receive this training for several years, but a crisis loomed every time we packed our bags. Once it was appendicitis, another time Ben's birth, and so forth. We were excited to finally be here. The training was incredible. We bonded well with our fellow students and worked hard on our assignments.

We had been staying in a guesthouse in Abidjan for almost two weeks when we were shocked to hear that Côte d'Ivoire (the Ivory Coast) had bombed some French soldiers in the northern part of the country. Should we leave? That was the question weighing on all of our minds. A Nigerian pastor was in the training with us. He immediately caught a flight out, telling us that our embassy would get us out but that he would be stuck in Abidjan if anything happened. The decision was made to continue our training, so we stayed put. We stocked up on groceries and filled many containers with water and rather anxiously waited to see what would happen.

Saturday was a fairly normal day. We went shopping in our neighborhood and planned a cookout that evening. Yet there was a feeling of impending disaster, and none of us could go to sleep. Even the kids were still milling around at ten p.m. We had heard sporadic gunfire and reports of looting in town during the day. Then suddenly the guesthouse manager ran up to our house and told us to get behind as many locked doors as we could. There was a mob coming, and the security forces had been unable to contain it.

The men locked the main doors and then the hallway door. Then the two of us wives were locked into a room at the far end of the hall with all eight children. Our husbands, John and Fred, stayed in the hallway with several butcher knives to try to defend us. We could hear the mob getting closer and closer. All along I had felt we were safe because the rebels and soldiers alike knew we were not politically involved. But a mob gone mad . . . there is no reasoning and no mercy. One little girl was asleep in bed, but as the shooting picked up we were afraid to leave her there in case a round of gunfire came through the window. Both of us moms were trying to keep the babies quiet in a vain hope that the mob wouldn't find us. The little girl woke up confused and afraid, so my daughters held her and comforted her. Another missionary kid, Noah, was only three years old. He was scared, and we couldn't quiet him down. Finally he let "big Christopher" hold him. It also helped calm Christopher to have someone he was responsible for.

We quietly prayed and encouraged each other with Bible verses, but we were terrified. We heard a number of loud explosions, and then attack helicopters began to drop what looked like balls of fire into the crowd. The gunfire became more insistent and closer, but finally the noise of the mob died away. Our husbands came and let us out of the room, and we went to our own rooms. There was still a lot of automatic weapons fire, so the kids and I slept in a tangled heap on the floor.

We lived through that night. The next day we learned that McCory, the neighborhood we were staying in, was the only neighborhood that had not been ransacked by the mobs. Some claim that a Lebanese doctor paid the mob leaders to protect our neighborhood. Others claim that because of its location with only one entrance, the soldiers were better able to protect us. I believe that those things may have been factors, but God in his mercy chose to protect us. His hand is mighty to save.

What about you? God can grant you sleep in even the most difficult situation. Put your trust fully in God and let him give you rest. Truly he is our protector.

Missionary Prayer Point: Political situations can change overnight. Pray for peace in countries where missionaries you know are working. Pray that when the crisis comes they would be perfectly at peace, knowing that God is protecting them.

Escape from Abidjan

> When I am afraid, I will trust in you. In God, whose word I praise, in God I trust; I will not be afraid. What can mortal man do to me?
>
> Psalm 56:3–4

We got up the next morning relieved to be alive. As we began listening to news reports, the realization hit us that we were too late. We had missed the window of opportunity, and now there was no way out of the country. There were still skirmishes being fought at the airport, so it was closed to civilian traffic. It was dangerous to leave our neighborhood because of the mobs that roamed freely. The French military had our neighborhood secured. Every so often an armored car with a machine gun mounted on the roof would cruise by the guesthouse. Well-armed soldiers had a very visible presence, but we still felt like prisoners.

All of us on the compound were missionaries, but outside of that fact we had very little in common. Some of us had large families, others were single and had no families. Some were young, others were older. Some were very extroverted and verbal about their fears, others were quiet and withdrawn. Yet we were all anxious and concerned about when and how we would get out of Abidjan.

The Ivorian soldiers cut the water supply for one day, and that became a point of tension. It was potentially a very volatile situation in which there could have been a lot of bickering and quarreling. There were definitely some tense moments, but we managed to live at peace with each other. One way I dealt with the stress was by cooking. Most afternoons I would bake a cake or some sort of dessert and deliver some to everyone.

Every afternoon most of the missionary women would sit in the yard and watch the kids play. With sixteen children (eight of these children were living in one "house," but we were all surrounded by the same outside wall and shared the same compound) there was no way to stay indoors all the time. Then Christopher came running to me, screaming, "That man is going to shoot me!" We had neighbors of another nationality who had a three-story building overlooking our compound. They had been very helpful all week, offering to use their contacts if we needed medication and offering physical protection with their weapons. We would often hear them shooting at night, although we had no idea who or what they were shooting. Then they began to feel restless on their compound and started doing target practice on the roof of their building. When they saw all our kids running around the yard, they decided that it would be entertaining to scare them. After they emptied their weapons at the target, they would point them at our kids and fire. Our children had no way of knowing the guns were empty, so they were terrified. We were obviously upset and concerned about the safety of our children. Our situation with the neighbors became almost as serious in our minds as the revolution going on around us.

All week long we would hear gunfire and see the attack helicopters hovering overhead. We would read the horror stories in the news and realize how well protected we were in our little enclave. Rumors flew back and forth. We knew both the American Embassy and our mission board were doing everything possible to get us out of the country, but it still wasn't safe to leave our area.

Wednesday, four days after the mob ransacking, we were told to pack a twenty-pound evacuation bag. There was a plane flying in for us that night. Then night fell and the plan changed.

"The plane can't get in here tonight. Tomorrow a cargo plane is coming, so go ahead and pack your suitcases."

Thursday morning dawned, and the mission directors and embassy personnel trying to arrange our evacuation still didn't know when we would get out. We did school that morning, and then I cooked lunch for my family. Right as I was calling everyone to eat, our leader came in and said, "You've got five minutes to pack ten pounds of stuff in a carry-on, and we are leaving!" Five minutes! How do you decide what you will most need? The Bible and medicine went in first. Then I told each of my older kids, "Don't pack any toys—just pack several sets of clothes and your Game Boy." I knew they would need something at the airport to entertain themselves.

I didn't even get a chance to check the bags. We ran out the door to the van. At the last minute someone told me to get water since there might not be anything at the airport. Once the van was underway Rebekah turned to me and confessed, "I packed my very special Legos. They don't weigh much and I couldn't leave them. They are special to me."

We were a very frightened and sedate group as our vans pulled into the neighborhood. We had no idea what we would see. We were shocked at how the landscape had changed in one week. The malls and stores where we had shopped the week before were shattered and looted. There were hulks of burned vehicles everywhere and signs of violence. The road to the airport was well guarded with tanks and soldiers all along the way. As we pulled onto the airport property, we had to drive through a maze of military vehicles and road blocks. The entire lawn of the airport was covered with razor wire. The kids immediately said, "Dad, this looks just like Normandy. Cool!" We had been afraid that the trip to the airport and seeing all the destruction would be traumatic to our kids, but they were fascinated with the soldiers, uniforms, weapons, and military vehicles.

We could see signs of fighting even at the airport. The doors had bullet holes in them. We went into the airport to begin our wait. We learned that it was the German Air Force that was getting us out. By now everyone was hungry, and all our food had been left on the table as we tried to pack and leave quickly. Another missionary had put all our sandwiches in a bag and brought them, so we all shared them. A bit later the Germans came through and gave our kids Rice Krispies Treats. The kids were all so tired and hungry, and I have never been so thankful for a treat. We had to laugh at the German news agency as they photographed the American refugees eating their treats in the Abidjan airport.

After several hours we were told that all the passengers had arrived and we could begin boarding. Family by family the soldiers brought us forward and searched us and our luggage. Then we walked out on the tarmac and loaded ourselves onto the Luftwaffe (German Air Force) plane that was waiting for us. The soldiers were such a help. They brought juice to everyone and even a toy to the baby who was getting very restless. Yet it was bizarre to me to see so many guns openly carried on the plane.

As we sat on the tarmac waiting for takeoff, it finally became real. We really were getting out of there. We were going to escape this madness.

One soldier was making small talk and asked me where I would go once they dropped us off in Ghana. "Oh, we're going back to Togo."

A look of horror crossed his face. "You mean you're not leaving Africa?"

"Oh no, our life and work are here. Our home is in Togo. We'll be fine there." He gave me a look that clearly said, "After all we've done to evacuate you, you don't even have the sense to get out of Africa?"

The flight to Accra, Ghana, was very quick and short. The German ambassador boarded our plane to welcome us and said, "Welcome to a safe place." We all wanted to weep at those words. At last we were truly safe.

What about you? If you were given five minutes to pack, what would you carry? What is most important to you? Take a close look at your priorities and think about what the essentials really are. Truly God is our refuge and we can find safety and security in him.

Missionary Prayer Point: Pray for missionaries as they deal with memories of traumatic events. Pray that God would bring healing and peace to them.

The Least of These

> Then the righteous will answer him, "Lord, when did we see you hungry and feed you, or thirsty and give you something to drink? When did we see you a stranger and invite you in, or needing clothes and clothe you? When did we see you sick or in prison and go to visit you?"
>
> The King will reply, "I tell you the truth, whatever you did for one of the least of these brothers of mine, you did for me."
>
> Matthew 25:37–40

Two doctors, an EMT, a nurse, and various medical personnel had come from the United States to help us run a week of free clinics in Natitingou, Benin. In spite of our best efforts, the scene was chaotic. We could treat about five hundred patients in a day, but for every person we saw, two new patients showed up. People were at the windows and doors clamoring to be seen, and quite a few people were sitting at the various medical stations in the process of being treated. Then Phoebe, the director of a local orphanage, arrived with ten of the sickest babies from her orphanage. One man in line began to object to the babies being seen first, but every woman in line turned to him and began vociferously correcting him and letting him know just how sick those children were. We left one line open to treat general patients, and the rest of us turned our attention to the orphans.

They were a pitiful sight—tiny and malnourished with wizened features and distended abdomens. They were ill with malaria, parasites, and other infections. Three babies were desperately ill and received injections. My twelve-year-old daughter, Sarah, was helping interpret and trying to get the weakest babies to drink formula from a syringe. She tenderly held them and cared for them like a professional, instead of like the preteen that she actually was.

The next day Phoebe returned with the three sickest babies so they could receive a repeat injection. One was in distress and didn't appear to have a chance to survive. The physician started an IV, and one of the nurses held the fragile baby all afternoon, doing everything possible. By late afternoon it was obvious that he was beyond our help. In spite of everything, he was only breathing eight times a minute. As a team, we gathered together, prayed, and wept over this little one. Sarah Joy and I held each other and grieved over this little life that would soon be lost. Phoebe carried him home, and that evening he died.

I honestly believed that we could have saved that baby's life. We had American doctors and medicines and a sincere desire to help people. Yet God holds the power of life and death in the palm of his hand.

When I realized that baby was going to die, my first thought was for my daughter. I wished she hadn't been there, hadn't gotten attached, didn't have to experience this grief. Later as we grieved together, I realized that yes, it was a painful experience for her, but it was also an opportunity for growth and maturity.

Ultimately, all we can do is reach out in love and show the compassion of Christ to those around us. True healing can come only from him.

What about you? What are you doing for the least of these? There are many legitimate organizations caring for the orphans of the world. You could get involved by praying for a specific child, giving financially to help support a child, or going to another country and caring for some of the children yourself. Don't be afraid of what may happen. Get involved and do what you can.

Missionary Prayer Point: Missionaries experience many heart-wrenching circumstances on a daily basis. Pray that God would keep their hearts tender and that they would not grow callous to the suffering around them.

Miss Manners Does Togo

> Love is patient, love is kind. It does not envy, it does not boast, it is not proud. It is not rude.
>
> 1 Corinthians 13:4–5

Manners. Good manners are important to any mother, but what do you do when you are living in another country with completely different standards of what constitutes good manners? Once when we were getting ready to go back to the United States, I looked around the dinner table. My children were very politely and neatly scooping up rice from their bowls with their fingers. I explained that we were headed to America, and in America one did not eat rice with one's fingers. All I got were looks of disbelief. After all, what else would one eat rice with?

One of the basics of good manners is learning to express thankfulness. That is a value that should transcend any culture. It has always been very important to me to teach my children to be grateful for all that we are given, but sometimes being grateful is a stretch.

One day we were sitting in a village compound, watching the village children play with some baby birds. I pitied these birds being away from their mothers. They were the most hideous creatures I had ever seen. They were almost completely naked, with a few straggly feathers trying to sprout. They were ungainly and had huge beaks. I knew these orphaned birds wouldn't survive long. Imagine my chagrin when the children in a very kind move gave each of my children one of these birds. "Sarah, Rebekah, and Christopher, don't forget to say thank you for the buzzards!" Saying thank you with a straight face would get them extra points.

One Sunday we had a church dedication, a baptism, and a dinner on the church grounds all in the same day. There were rain clouds building, and it was miserably hot and steamy. Our family drove an hour and a half in a crowded vehicle over bumpy roads to get to church.

We were thankful to see that the church was crowded, but when there are that many people in a small tin-roofed building, it is like a sauna. Still, we had a very good service. The highlight of it was when John threw a rock out of the window hole to illustrate a point. Ben thought that looked like fun and threw his own rock, hitting the chief!

After the church service was over, we drove to a nearby cow pond. We hiked through the straggly grass and waded through the herd of cows to the site chosen for the baptism. We watched as several new converts were baptized, then we drove back to the church.

While we were gone some of the women had prepared a meal. All my children were really hungry and making bets about what they hoped was fixed for lunch. The first thing we were offered was non-fermented homemade beer in a calabash (half of a hollowed-out gourd used for drinking). John told the kids, "It's not alcoholic. This is sort of like a Coke." Sarah said, "Don't believe him—this does not taste like Coke!" John stoically guzzled his whole calabash and for his trouble was given a second bowlful.

Then the women brought our food. It was rice and spaghetti with red sauce, which, fortunately, is my children's favorite of any village food. It was accompanied by a portion of mystery meat, and that was the moment when I realized that my children had finally mastered the art of eating in the village. Sarah had realized that no one around her could understand her words, but they clearly understood her tone of voice and facial expressions. So with a pleasant smile and a polite tone of voice, she said,

"Mom, they have served me part of the stomach tied up in the intestines. I know it is a special treat, but do I have to eat it?"

I realized that my child had mastered manners in Togo, because she was willing to eat the intestines if necessary and not say "Yuck!" or make any kind of a face when served this "tasty" treat. Fortunately, she didn't have to eat it. Here we did not have to clean our plates to be considered polite. In fact, it is polite to leave some food for the children to eat. (Normally guests and the men eat first. The women eat separately, and whatever is left over is fed to the children. Families don't normally eat together like in America's culture.) So Sarah left her "treat" on her plate, and we all enjoyed our meal.

Having good manners is so much more than knowing what fork to use. The heart of good manners is love and considering others instead of yourself. That principle works no matter what culture you are dealing with!

What about you? Sometimes it is easy to get into sloppy habits with those we love most. How are your manners at home with your family? Do you make an effort to be kind and polite, or are you rude and rushed in your daily dealings with your loved ones? Make a concerted effort to show loving consideration toward those around you. Live with a grateful heart.

Missionary Prayer Point: Pray that missionaries would have a grateful heart for every gift—buzzards and all!

Houdini the Parrot

> I will instruct you and teach you in the way you should go; I will counsel you and watch over you.
>
> Psalm 32:8

Houdini was originally named Skittles because of his bright plumage. He was a Senegalese green parrot with bright green feathers and some orange, yellow, and red markings. He didn't talk, but he could screech and squawk quite nicely. John loved listening to him in the mornings because, as he said, "It makes me feel like I'm in Africa." Somehow I knew I was in Africa without the parrot, but we did enjoy his racket.

This parrot had a penchant for escaping (hence the name change to Houdini). The first time we found the cage locked and the bird hopping around the yard, we thought the guard had accidentally let Houdini out and then had shut the door so we wouldn't blame him.

We decided the catch on the door must not work well, so we locked the door with a bunch of wire. Later we would find the door securely locked, but the parrot would be hopping around the yard, screaming for help. Then we realized that he must somehow have squeezed between the bars on the cage. We covered the whole cage in chicken wire. That held him for about a week, but then he chewed a hole through the wire and escaped again.

Unfortunately, we have a bird dog named Hoosier, so every time the parrot got loose, Hoosier thought he was in heaven. The tips of Houdini's wings were clipped so he couldn't fly. We would hear a commotion and go outside to find the bird running and squawking for dear life and the dog gleefully chasing him around the yard.

This bird had a spacious cage, a swing, and lots of fresh food and water, but he was sure the outside world was a better place. Yet the only thing that awaited him outside the cage was death by dog. You can guess what happened. One day Hoosier beat us to Houdini.

I don't want to end up like Houdini. Too often we perceive being in God's will like being in a cage. We see all sorts of bright, appealing things out in the world, and we leave the safety of God's plan to pursue them. We discover emptiness and disillusionment when we pursue our own ends instead of waiting on God.

Right now we are at a crossroads as we wait on God. For the first time in our adult lives, we really desire to move back to the United States to live permanently. We sense God is leading us in that direction, but he keeps saying, "Not yet. Wait on me. Watch and see what I will do."

In the aftermath of the Abidjan coup, one of my children struggled with post-traumatic stress, and we wanted to leave for America. For weeks he had nightmares, became very aggressive, and couldn't function at school or home. He went from having many African friends to being terrified of them. "What's going to stop those bad men from coming here?" was his cry. Even though we knew it wasn't time to leave yet, we wanted to pack up our suitcases and go home. After all, in America there are grandparents, schools, children's programs at church—and no military coups.

Now I am thankful that we didn't imitate Houdini and leave abruptly. My child is happy here again. The nightmares are gone, he is playing with his friends again, and he is dealing with day-to-day life. When we do leave, he will be left with happy memories of friends and a place he loves.

I once thought we would spend the rest of our lives in Africa. Now I realize that God is gradually leading us back to

America. He has promised to guide us and be our counselor. I am choosing to trust him to lead us step by step the rest of the way home.

What about you? How do you make decisions? Don't make your decisions hastily without prayer. Take time to seek God's face and follow his leading step by step. He has only good plans for you.

Missionary Prayer Point: Pray that missionaries would seek God's face in every decision they make. Pray that they would choose to act in accordance with his will.

Suzanne Crocker grew up as a missionary kid in Central America. She attended Samford University in Birmingham, Alabama, where she studied to become a nurse. She and her husband have four children and were missionaries with the International Mission Board of the Southern Baptist Convention for more than ten years. They currently reside in Huntsville, Alabama.